I DID IT MY WAY

I DID IT MY WAY

BIKRAM DASGUPTA

RUPA

Published by
Rupa Publications India Pvt. Ltd 2018
7/16, Ansari Road, Daryaganj
New Delhi 110002

Sales centres:
Bengaluru Chennai
Hyderabad Jaipur Kathmandu
Kolkata Mumbai Prayagraj

Copyright © Bikram Dasgupta, 2018
Photographs courtesy: Bikram Dasgupta

The views and opinions expressed in this book are the author's own and
the facts are as reported by him which have been verified to the extent possible,
and the publishers are not in any way liable for the same.

P-ISBN: 978-81-291-5076-9
E-ISBN: 978-81-291-5077-6

Fourth impression 2024

10 9 8 7 6 5 4

The moral right of the author has been asserted.

Printed in India

I dedicate this book to two of my prized hopes, inspirations and aspirations as I look forward in my life further. They have been the biggest motivation for me in my life.

My sons, Rahul and Romit.

Contents

Author's Note

I have been somewhat of an enigma to most people that I have crossed paths with in the three decades of professional and entrepreneurial journey, including my immediate family and friends.

I have meant different things to different people at various stages of my long and eventful journey and this brings me to the most vexing of questions that have come my way; particularly from those who form my inner circle: 'What is the residual value of what you have done?' and 'Where do you go from here?'

Coming from a sedate Bengali middle-class family, one endowed with large measures of creative energy, my life has been an assimilation of learning that I have consciously and unconsciously picked up along my journey. If my first gurus in entrepreneurship were the innocuous Chhedi and Sadhu from my Indian Institute of Technology Kharagpur (IIT KGP) days, I found great scholarship in the late Amit Datta Gupta and sharpened my street smart by following the late Dadan Bhai.

In all I tend to see myself as a risk-taker rather than any one boxed definition of an entrepreneur. Is there a learning to be had from there? Sure is, if one were to carefully weigh in the brinkmanship; something that comes along the risk-taking package.

I have also been a firm believer in the power behind well thought out maxims. To me they hold life's great lessons and have given me the power to keep focused and not stray from my path at times of deep distress.

Of all the maxims that are close to my heart, Thomas A. Edison's famous quote, 'Most of my ideas belong to people who didn't bother to develop them', is perhaps something that I identify myself closest with. I have, in life, strived to string together diverse and asynchronous dots into a story. A narrative that has gone on to become an entrepreneurial edifice, some successful and some that died an early death.

Who then is to measure risk and how do we define success?

These and a myriad other thoughts prodded me to put pen to paper. Perhaps (and I dearly hope) my readers will find within these pages that they hold, the singular and unifying 'tick' that makes me tick. Perhaps they will discover the residual value of what I leave behind, and that it is not always foolhardy to take risks that some would scoot away from. They will also perhaps glean that learning can be had from diverse sources and find merit in Thomas A. Edison's quote in their own life journeys.

As I enter my sunset years, I look forward to investing my time and energy to help budding entrepreneurs find their feet and soar with their dreams. My newest brand 'BDG Global', I hope, will help me fulfil this aspiration.

Those of you who wish to talk to me about the book or on subjects beyond the book can look me up at *www.bikramdasgupta.com* or write to me at *bdg@bikramdasgupta.com*.

Innocence

One

GETTING INTO IIT KHARAGPUR GAVE ME a sense of achievement and brought about a fierce sense of independence. It fuelled in me an urge to do well for myself.

For the first time in my life, I was surrounded by people who excelled at almost anything that they put their minds to. They pushed you and they pushed you hard. I found the experience uplifting; it drove me to excel in areas that were close to my heart. I didn't understand it then. It dawned on me, much later in life, the reason for my yearning to push myself into things that I found close to my heart.

IIT brought home to me the value of freedom. I started appreciating what Ma meant when she, in her own affable way, quoted Eleanor Roosevelt. 'Freedom,' she went on to say, 'makes a huge requirement of every human being. With freedom comes responsibility. For the person who is unwilling to grow up, the person who does not want to carry his own weight, this is a frightening prospect.' Ma knew how to time her messages well.

It was also a time of pure happiness and learning life's lessons. IIT reaffirmed my belief that there was life beyond books. Life's great lessons sprung not from lecture halls but from the fierce hall competitions and the thrill of winning; the ability to roll up your sleeves and an unbridled urge to triumph over the odds; the unfettering of your creative instincts and thinking beyond the square box; looking up to the prodigies, not in envy, but searing in you the promise to measure up to the best.

To me, being in IIT was singularly important not because it was and still is identified as an academic seat of learning—an institution of excellence—but for the 'life' that it offered me and the various pathways to self-development. It let me explore, enjoy and ultimately manage the 'freedom' that it offered in the midst of its daily regimentation and the doors that it opened for me to discover and nurture the natural 'talent' that all of us are endowed with.

Abhindra eased my entry into life at IIT. Still a year senior, he made sure word got around that we were friends, and I perhaps escaped with much milder doses of ragging compared to my fellow batchmates.

A multifaceted chap, Abhindra excelled in debates, elocutions, recitations and acting. Lanky, sharp-looking and bursting with energy, he could charm his way into a person's heart. He had a way with words. Few, if any, could say 'no' to his face.

Abhindra had met me at the railway station, and a warm hug later escorted me to the campus. He also had a surprise in store. True to style, on receiving my postcard, Abhindra took it upon himself to ensure that I was allotted a room in the same hostel and block that he was in. By the time I arrived, Abhindra had charmed his way up and down the administrative labyrinth. His was an act of camaraderie and thoughtfulness that I was forever grateful for.

The eight souls occupying C-Block, First Floor, West Wing of RP Hall found themselves an additional boarder and the newly christened 'Nonagon' took up residence in a row of adjacent rooms that opened up to a long-columned corridor and a lifelong bond of friendship.

My room was, by design, next to Abhindra's, all set firmly in the midst of busy traffic. All manner of characters trooped past or chose to walk in—never mind the time of day or night—enveloping one in a constant buzz of human chatter, except during the dead heat of the summers or when classes were on in full swing. An eerie silence hung over the corridors then. It seemed as if the crickets had suddenly lost their voice.

Of the Nonagon that lorded over C-Block, First Floor, West Wing, Shyamal Bandopadhyay had, early on, donned the mantle of a leader and we throve in his charge. An avid football player, Shyamal was of a stocky build and had a plucky personality to match. Born into a cultured, middle-class Bengali family from Belgharia, a suburb on the northern end of Calcutta (Kolkata), famous for its stockily built men who feared nothing and were quick to temper, Shyamal was every bit the 'Belgharia' character.

Shyamal carried on him a *bhujali*, sheathed in a smart leather case. The dagger resembled a Nepalese kukri in design and form. Shyamal's prized possession had an ornately designed handle with a gleaming steel blade to finish off its mean look. It quickly became known that you didn't want to mess with Shyamal, especially when he had his bhujali for company.

Apart from Abhindra, affectionately rechristened as *Lambu* or the tall one, and Shyamal, Nonagon comprised Siddhartha (Sherry), Amitabha (Hazra), Apurba (Apu), Bidhu, Hitendu and Nirbhar. I was the youngest of them, the others being a year senior to me, but was never made to feel so.

Hazra was famous for his long bouts of sleep (his sharp intellect needed that); nothing seemed to bother him as he slept, child-like, through the commotion in the hallway. Hitendu was the unchallenged carom champion; Nirbhar was the mathematical genius—the go-to person when we found ourselves battling with some mind-boggling mathematical puzzle, the solution seeming to eternally evade us; Sherry was the balanced soul managing to bring sanity and purpose to our restless young souls.

Apu and Bidhu were lucky enough to be allotted a large double-bedded room, which eventually became our adda room. Most of us spent our spare time in their room, only to stagger to our quarters to crash out in the wee hours of the morning.

There was phenomenal learning to be had from each of the Nonagon characters. As I reflect back, I realise how Shyamal's risk-taking ability influenced me as much as I was drawn by Sherry's penchant for meticulousness or the ability to keep one's worries and aches by the wayside as one tried sleeping as child-like as Hazra.

స

Two

COMING FROM THE DUSTY, SEMI-INDUSTRIAL town of Durgapur, I had instantly fallen in love with the sprawling IIT KGP campus and its huge expanses of greenery. I loved the serenity of its surroundings and tree-lined pathways. I felt at peace with myself.

It didn't take long for me to discover that life at IIT KGP had a pace quite its own. It swung widely from frantic—during the examination season—only to fall back to its usual laid-back pace and come to a dead halt during the long and passionate *adda* sessions.

IIT KGP's laid-back pace, however, was a perfect veneer to its daily regimentation. You had to wake up early, at about 6 a.m. As you queued up for the morning shower, strains of Harry Belafonte's *Jamaica Farewell* would start wafting in from the shower stalls, reaching its crescendo at '*My heart is down, my head is turning around, I had to leave a little girl in Kingston Town...*' Staying in bed meant you hardly stood any chance of having breakfast, which invariably cleared itself out by 8 a.m., missing, as Ma would grumble, 'the most important meal of the day.'

On most days, morning classes were done by 11.30 a.m. and we found our way back to the residential hall, making a beeline for Sadhu's stall. A languid lunch later, we trudged back for the remaining classes of the day.

Surreptitiously tucked away under the staircase of RP Hall, Sadhu's stall stocked much-needed cigarettes, cakes, biscuits and an assortment of snacks. Summer months saw Sadhu, an astute, business-minded fellow, stocking up on cold beverages and his much-loved mango lassi.

Sadhu was no mendicant as his name belied. He kept his stall open only during lunch breaks, away from the gaze of higher authorities and quickly dispensed with business, all within a span of an hour, leaving no trace of a heaving and bustling marketplace of outstretched arms.

Each one of us had a running *khatta* (line of credit) with Sadhu on a 'payable-when-able' basis. Forever a benign credit extender, Sadhu had, in true entrepreneurial spirit, built enduringly strong bonds of friendship with the meagre posse of postmen who ferried us our money orders from home and was the first to know of the smallest of inward remittances cycling down the gates of the campus.

On those days, you could expect an early evening courtesy call from the man himself, sweetly pleading if some of the bulging credit could be squared off. Sadhu never rung you dry, but had his own notion of the length of the credit rope that could be unrolled for each one of us.

◆

A few months into our new lives, we started loathing the regimented food of the hall mess. Sundays were particularly galling. The Sunday chicken stew became a running joke; it came with oodles of watery and worryingly inconsistent gravy. One had to embark upon a serious fishing expedition to locate small chunks of chicken that lay buried under the murky gravy pool.

One particular Saturday evening, as we sat huddled in Apu and Bidhu's room, perennially hungry as young persons are, Shyamal took it upon himself to get us out of the conundrum. Shyamal trooped down the hallway, with a few of us in tow, and presented himself before Chatterjee Babu at his abode on the ground floor.

A docile and timid gentleman, Chatterjee Babu was a quintessential Bengali bhadralok who ran his contractual canteen at RP Hall—one that he had strategically placed at the entrance of the hall mess.

A stickler for neatness, Shyamal took over the menu—a witness to many a yellowed thumb—and drew a perfectly straight line besides the price listing. He then proceeded to write C-BLOCK—FIRST FLOOR—WEST WING—PRICE LIST in block letters at the head of the freshly minted column and insouciantly slashed all prices by half.

'This,' he said, turning over the menu to a dumbstruck Chatterjee Babu, 'will be the pricelist for C-Block, First Floor, West Wingers, till further notice.' As he strode off, he added in the general direction of

Chatterjee Babu, 'Dues shall be squared off at the end of each month, as and when money comes from home.'

Chatterjee Babu, who was heavily perspiring by now, saw the futility in joining issue with Shyamal and left it upon fate and, maybe his karma, to bear the loss while Nonagon roosted itself in C-Block, First Floor, West Wing.

On our part, we kept our side of the bargain and almost eschewed the hall mess for good and it befell upon Chatterjee Babu and his boy to feed us lunch and dinner and at times conjure up dishes that didn't figure on his yellow-thumbed menu.

In time, Chatterjee Babu's kitchen yielded some of the zingiest aloo parathas and bhajis that titillated our young taste buds compared to the morbid curries dished out at the hall mess.

❧

Three

OUR EVENINGS WERE ALMOST EXCLUSIVELY reserved for sports and outdoor activities. Most of us played some form of sport or the other rather than sit idle.

I was a permanent fixture in the hall common room and revelled in playing table tennis—TT for short. We played with abandon, without a care in the world. Apart from the usual, we played what was coined as 'round table tennis'. Any number of players could play as we scurried along the table, trying not to miss a shot until only two were left to finish off the game.

If I longed to dwell in the twilight zone of being part-introvert, part-extrovert, I found myself hurtling down unfamiliar tracks. I was early into my second year when I, goaded by my mates, took up a challenge with the hall TT champion Gittu Ghosh—whom we all referred to as Gittu da—who was then in his final year at IIT KGP.

As perhaps with all seniors he took to the game casually, humouring a junior, and ended up losing the first round. He struck back with ferocity in the second round, flipping and smashing the ball while I did my best to face the onslaught with chops and blocks, prevailing over my opponent by the slenderest of margins. From then on it was all downhill for the champion as desperation and frustration got the better of him. Word quickly got around of a lanky left-handed rookie beating the hall champion, ending up in earning a place for me in the hall TT team.

We were over with dinner by 8 p.m. and went about for a stroll within the vast campus grounds, the moonlight flirting in and out of the tree-lined boulevards. Our evening walks were also synonymous with Chhedi's, an institution for all IIT KGP students, past and present. We frequented Chhedi's through the night and early morning, the last of the stragglers heaving themselves off to bed as late as four in the morning.

Born in Gorakhpur, Uttar Pradesh, Chhedi, or Anwar Khan, as he was debuted by his parents, was a teenager when he decided to follow his father to the still under construction IIT KGP site in 1961. A resourceful lad, he quickly set up a small tea shop next to the low perimeter wall at the entrance of the main campus and before long became a must stopover for all students.

Chhedi kept his ramshackle establishment operational 24×7 and performed the duties of a provider and a common man's therapist with equal aplomb. He soothed frayed nerves and deftly navigated through the mood swings of a student. To a first-year student he would quip, '*Kuch hi dino ki baat hai* (it's just a matter of days),' after a bout of harmless ragging, at times in the dead of the night, making the youngster feel at ease.

Dennis, Chhedi's Man-Friday, was the go-to guy. He took your orders, mopped up the table after you, and made you feel part of a fine-dining experience. You were scarcely settled before Dennis—Cheddi's mobile menu card—rattled off the day's menu at a bewildering speed, expecting a speedier response before presenting himself to the next batch of hungry guests. For all the years that I was at IIT KGP, I never saw Dennis lose his smile while he juggled between chatting you up, taking orders, serving, mopping and settling dues. His happiness and hero-like demeanour was infectious.

We huddled at Chhedi's at all odd hours taking long-drawn sips of chai, a Wills Navy Cut cigarette stuck between our fingers discussing anything and everything under the sun. We held grudges against our professors for their unmitigated tyranny, or the travesty of justice when a comrade was axed out early from an afternoon class; the poor fellow's only fault lay in grazing heavily against the professor—while being thoroughly sozzled—during the professor's morning jogging spree.

Compared to hall food, Chhedi's was, for some, a fine-dining restaurant. We would swear by his *tinku* (bun stuffed with an omelette and sprinkled with a fair dose of spicy red masala), aloo and veg chops. His monthly credit system ensured that we were well fed during the month, but gave rise to an entirely different set of challenges when we had to dial home for funds.

Between Sadhu and Chhedi's, we were given our first great lessons on entrepreneurship. They taught us, however banal it might sound, that customers always came first. The ability to bond with your customers, who in time came looking for more than the sum of the wares that one peddled, was paramount to an enterprise's success. They gave us rich pointers on fiscal prudence and the uncanny ability to mop up our credit lines before they morphed into worthless shreds of paper.

In Sadhu and Chhedi, I saw reflected my need for independence; to feel as though I was in charge of my destiny, which augured well with my rebellious urge to stand out.

As I reflect back, I realise how much of an influence Sadhu and Chhedi had in identifying with my own latent entrepreneurial instincts. They were my first gurus in the art of entrepreneurship and were perhaps the best inspirational models to have at that impressionable age.

∽

Four

INTER-HALL COMPETITIONS AND THE SPRING FEST were times of great fervour at IIT KGP—something that I believe still is. These were our gladiatorial arenas, fiercely competitive, and marked by the spilling of copious amounts of creative blood. We bayed to outdo each other and by the fairest of means.

Spring Fest, or SF as everyone chose to term it, gave me a first-hand experience of the mechanics and planning that went into organising mass events.

Spring Fest was a revelation to me and I filed away every little detail. It brought out the best and worst in a person…if you had alpha males take up leadership roles with poor execution skills, then you had avowed introverts who bagged some of the biggest sponsorships. I spent hours on end at the open-air theatre—TOAT for those familiar with IIT KGP and its lay—seeing people come alive, marvelling, if not envious, of the spectrum of talent that abounded.

On the other hand, with 11 competing halls and events spread out over two whole weeks, inter-hall competitions were much fiercer and involving. We let loose our creative instincts and vied to romp home with the top honours.

Hall competitions entailed contesting in three distinct events. The first two events with a duration of 15 minutes each, comprised a group song and western music. Time was the clincher and halls were judged on how well they managed time and simultaneously come up with a brilliant performance since one had all of 15 minutes for the stage set-up, performance and finally dismantling the stage.

The third act comprised of hall music for which we were doled out a whole 45 minutes. With time management already adjudged in the previous two acts, we were more relaxed and came up with some scintillating jamboree of Indian and western music ensembles carefully chosen to sway the crowds.

On my part, I enjoyed the rush of adrenaline that went into competing in the group song and western music sections. With time at a premium, success meant meticulous planning, thinking out of the box and flawless, military-style, execution.

We spent hours on end at Chhedi's discussing and hotly debating the minutest of details. Each of us were handed charge of different aspects of the event and were given a posse of helpers to execute it. It usually fell on us and our team to design, put up and dismantle the stage. The more musically endowed among us took on the burden of swaying the crowds with their performances.

In one such annual hall competition, we happened to select *Megha Re Bole Jhanan* for the group song section, from the wildly popular 1959 Hindi romantic comedy *Dil Deke Dekho* starring Shammi Kapoor and Asha Parekh. Shot in the backdrop of a heavily laden sky in the cool climes of a hill station, with Shammi Kapoor sensuously crooning to his lady love, the song had all the right 'masala' to get the crowd to their feet.

The challenge lay in creating a backdrop and stage setting that mimicked the real thing—at least as close as possible. Clouds came easily, but what about creating rain? How does one create the shimmering effect of a light drizzle? We couldn't possibly drag a shower and drench the stage!

We tossed and rejected ideas at an alarming rate before we came up with a somewhat unique proposition. We decided to build a composite stage backdrop handy enough to be lugged on and off stage within our allotted time.

The backdrop mimicked the cloudy climes of a hill station—all elements hand-painted. For the drizzle effect, we ran fine dark threads of coir diagonally across the entire frame of the backdrop. The coir threads were interspersed with round blobs of white paper at regular intervals and swayed gently by the draught generated by a slowly spinning fan—one that was naturally tucked out of sight. The rest was history.

The roots of my strong performance orientation and obsession with 'performance' in my later working life lay in the invaluable exposure to the Spring Fest and the fiercely contested hall competitions. The feeling of winning and walking away with the trophy was way better than wallowing for days on end for defeats suffered.

In the midst of winning and heart-wrenching losses, I picked up invaluable lessons on project management; delivering when it mattered the most, the value in rolling up one's sleeves and doing the smallest of tasks to perfection. It taught one to look deep within and tap into the innate reservoir of creativity and the ability to think beyond the mundane.

It also proved to me that life's greatest lessons were learnt not within the confines of the classrooms but the great outdoors such as coffee shops—which in our case was Chhedi's.

෴

Five

THE LONG YEARS AT IIT KGP finally came to an end. It arrived more quickly than any of us had expected or wished for. We spent the last few days packing up our little worlds and bidding adieu to friends, promising lifelong bonds of friendship and camaraderie.

I spent the next couple of months home in Durgapur enjoying the break from academics. I lazed around and did what pleased my fancy, rarely spending time at home. I did not see myself appearing for a master's programme and instead focused my energies on hunting for exciting work openings in some of the largest national and multinational companies.

I borrowed Baba's old Remington typewriter to type out my resume and covering letters. It took a considerable amount of paper before I was fully satisfied with the result, holding up the paper against the light and feeling good about it.

Winter had set in and it was on one of those early cold and foggy mornings that the postman delivered a registered letter addressed in my name. I held in my hands the answer to a fortnight of anxious anticipation. I tore into the envelope to reveal a stiffly formal letter requesting me to join Indian Oxygen as a trainee. I was advised to report to their headquarters at Taratala, Calcutta, for nine months of training, after which my final posting location would be 'intimated'. Indian Oxygen was a true-blue British company, now with Indians at the helm.

I remember feeling a deep sense of relief. Bengal, during the 1970s, was fast turning into a nightmare. Torching of buses, trams and sundry modes of public transport were commonplace, coupled with frequent rallies and processions that threw life out of gear for the citizens. Industry started leaving the state in droves as labour militancy grew by the day, forcing frequent lockouts and strikes. Those were uneasy times.

As the expansive Indian Oxygen headquarters loomed into view, I was reminded of what Ma had told me, years back, when I was to take the first of my many train rides to Kharagpur.

'Bikram,' she had said, with a great deal of urgency, 'In a few minutes, you will be on your way to a place where many persons will be better than you—or at least appear to be so. Don't get intimidated. You will cope, you will learn how—you have managed before and you always will. All I want is for you to remember this one thing as you go through life.'

She paused as her eyes bore into me. 'Listen to me. In the years ahead, if the world should contain just 10 people, I want it to be Bikram and nine others. If there are a 100, it should be Bikram and 99 others. You must be there—wherever there are persons who count, who make a difference.'

◆

As beginners, we were not only expected to be fully versed with various product lines, but also ingest a wide variety of technical information. We were trained to identify welding equipment and electrodes with their various compositions, detect gases correctly and the hazards associated with them. We were taken through elaborate sessions on safety and safe working practices which most of us, except for the guys eyeing production roles, largely yawned through.

We were about nine or 10 fresh graduates who were selected that particular year—to be later strewn across the country, in various capacities and functions. The training centre at Beliaghata, Calcutta, mimicked a fairly large factory floor and the instructors made sure that we were technically well accomplished to deal with all aspects of welding by the end of the training programme.

Mr R.C. Karmakar, our lead instructor, was a tough taskmaster. Having risen through the ranks, he took it upon himself to ensure that we went through every bit of the vast curricula with the zeal and earnestness that it deserved. We found ourselves back at school again, eagerly anticipating dispersal hour!

We were shepherded back to the Taratala headquarters for the last three, or maybe four, days of training with a farewell party thrown in on the last day. We were each handed a sealed envelope that detailed our posting location along with a one-way train ticket to the next destination. My ticket would take me to Madras (Chennai), where I would be stationed for the next four months, picking up the ropes, before I moved along to Visakhapatnam (Vizag)—my posting location. You had your choices made for you.

I offered to give a farewell speech on behalf of my batch, which fixed itself rather oddly to the regimented routine of farewell parties at Indian Oxygen. I presented five to seven lines on each of the instructors, with Mr Karmakar in the lead.

The farewell speech went down well with the crowd, catapulting me into the spotlight. Word must have travelled pretty fast since I increasingly got identified as one of the brighter ones in the batch.

Thus, I unwittingly did end up following Ma's advice to 'learn to identify yourself' and marvelled at the outcome of such an innocuous-sounding statement.

⌒⌒

Six

THE TAXI, A UBIQUITOUS AMBASSADOR, eased into the station's porch and came to an unsteady halt. 'That will be 22 rupees, sahib,' the driver muttered, as he leant across, noisily resetting the fare meter. I hurriedly paid off the cabbie, gladly stepping onto the muggy sunlit stairs of Howrah station. Anything was better than getting roasted in a cab while collecting the city's grime on your face.

I jostled through the teeming crowds before finding a spot to settle Ma down. I had her sit on the trunk, the holdall erect besides her—a worthy buffer against the milling crowds—as I elbowed my way back to join the queue at the enquiry window. It was the mid-1970s when trains were known to be notoriously late, no matter which side of the country one was off to.

I led Ma to the platform, the porter parting through the crowds, trunk and holdall neatly perched on his head, an arm extended to balance the precious load. Railway porters, I observed, have a fascinating gait unique to their tribe; they neither trot nor amble but settle for a pace in between.

The train finally drew into the station, sending a shiver of nervous chatter rippling through the platform. Chaos descended upon humanity as the passengers made a wild dash for the carriages; the able-bodied ones dragging their wife, kids and luggage in one clean sweep.

Coach and seat located, I went about securing my luggage with a thick chain and a large padlock to match. Ma had insisted on both. 'You can't be too careful with trains these days,' she said. 'You don't want to land up in Madras with no shoes or luggage, do you?' she had added with an air of finality. I wanted to say 'shoes!' but stopped short. Ma was always the more practical of my parents.

I stepped back onto the platform. It was time Ma caught a cab back home. I bent down and touched her feet, seeking her blessings. 'Take care and do well,' was all that she said.

She was not one to cry and make a fuss about me. Ma was a lady of few words. Ma lived beyond the mundane. To her, it was life's larger issues that mattered and captivated her imagination. Ma was a rarity, living by her instincts—looking beyond the obvious, searching for the core. She instilled in me an undying trait; to look beyond, outside the ordinary, the mundane, reinforcing the lessons learnt at IIT.

It was much later in life that Ma had confessed that she had suffered to see her youngest posted at the other end of our vast country. That was Ma.

I settled down, bracing myself for the long journey ahead, as the train ploughed its way through the shimmering haze of the afternoon heat. The heat, the chatter, the sudden speckles of soot flying through the window, nothing bothered me; I was excited at the prospect of getting started with life! No, I was not bustling with ideas or dreams of grandiose achievements. To crown it, I had no plans. I was a 20-something, excited to be earning my keep and looking forward to having a good time.

◆

It was late in the evening as the train finally chugged into Madras Central. I let the crowds ebb before stepping onto the platform, only to find porters in short supply. Finally, a lanky fellow presented himself and I took off running, trying not to lose sight of the fellow, as he wound his way to the auto-rickshaw stand.

I guess I must have looked every bit the out-of-town guy as I found myself mobbed by autodrivers, each eager for my fare. To my dismay, they decided, that very moment, that they could understand neither Hindi nor English, happily beleaguering me in Tamil, of which I knew not a syllable.

Salvation finally came in the form of a middle-aged autodriver who, taking plight at my predicament, shooed away the rest of the pack and offered to drive me to my destination. We settled on the fare over some fanatic gesticulations, and were off, tearing through the night streets of Madras.

I alighted at the entrance of a small lodge in Kodambakkam and paid off my 'saviour', his wide grin betraying the padded fare, despite all the finger stabbing in the night air.

A quick dinner later, I was off to bed, sleeping like a log through the night, the excitement and exhaustion of the last two days finally catching up.

I woke up with sunlight streaming through the windows, disoriented at my surroundings, sleeping on a strange bed flanked by unfamiliar furniture. It took me a few minutes to get my bearings in order.

A leisurely breakfast later, I was off exploring my immediate surroundings. It was a languid Sunday morning in Madras as the city woke up to its morning rituals. Residents made their way to the local market, while the more pious among them, having already finished their morning ablutions, their foreheads adorned with elaborate *tilaka*s, three horizontal streaks, followed by a red vermilion sphere, made their way back from their daily temple run, cupped hands full of bright flowers and ritual offerings made to their reigning deity.

I found it vaguely disconcerting that I couldn't understand the language spoken around me. Landing in a foreign city makes one realise the role that language plays in identifying with the culture and daily life of the city. You suddenly find yourself as Gulliver did, unable to fathom the tongue, while the world goes scurrying about you. Language binds you as readily as it puts the sea between you and your fellow beings.

I soon came across Liberty Theatre, a delightful two-storeyed structure with a semi-circular porch and a low perimeter wall. I was to later learn that it was one of the oldest movie theatres in Madras. I made a mental note of its location and promised to be back.

I was quite a movie buff and an avid Dev Anand fan. I swore by his penchant for nodding and rapid-fire dialogue delivery and revelled in mimicking his style, sending my friends into peals of laughter.

I was hugely influenced by Dev Anand and his predilection for reading and re-reading his scripts and dialogues and liberally correcting them till he had satisfied himself that they were worthy of taking to the stage. I marvelled at how the youth, and also to some measure the older generation, fell in love with the way he emoted and even the most outlandish of delivery styles had people swooning for him.

One of my all-time favourite Dev Anand dialogues, that I must have performed at countless get-togethers, was '*Paanch lakh ka maal aur puchehese hazzar inam, yeh koi mazaq hai...*' as I launched into his gait while rolling my hand, resulting in wild whoops from the audience.

My partiality towards Dev Anand was such that I unconsciously mirrored his gait and the way he styled his hair.

❦

Seven

A SHORT THIRTY-MINUTE TRAIN RIDE BROUGHT me to the Indian Oxygen Madras factory the following morning. Smaller than the Calcutta factory, it was located in the northern fringes of the city and was a desolate spot. With no human habitation in near sight, except for the occasional rumbling truck on the high road, which cut through the industrial zone, it was not a happening place to be in.

I presented myself to the receptionist, a middle-aged lady of serious disposition sitting ramrod straight, enveloped in an impregnable scent of jasmine that adorned her rich back tassel. Introductions dispensed with, I was led to a small sitting area, happy to be away from her matronly gaze. I later learnt her name—Prema—and discovered her to be quite a jovial character, belying her stoic exterior façade. She was always ready with a joke, most of which escaped me since she painstakingly transliterated them from Tamil to English, shearing them of their lustre.

I did not have to wait long before I was ushered into the capacious chamber of the regional manager (South)—the high priest who lorded over his flock sprinkled across major tracts of southern India. An extremely well-appointed gentleman with a rapidly balding pate, Mr A.K. Bhattacharya had a sonorous voice and an English diction that belied his Bengali roots.

Mr Bhattacharya rose from his perch and a warm handshake later ushered me to a well-cushioned chair opposite his perch. I sank into the soft fabric, feeling conscious of my long hair that seemed, in some measure, out of place in this temple with its high priest in attendance. But then it was fashionable to wear your hair long.

What followed was an exhaustive inquiry into my background, genealogy included. His eyes lit up when I mentioned my father, who was by now a well-recognised children's poet in his own right. For all the Bengali commonality, he never for once dropped his correct demeanour or launched into his native tongue. But he made you feel comfortable while happily prising away information.

An excellent listener, he didn't interrupt you midway as he sat back, relaxed, steepling his fingers, exuding an aura of confidence that brightened up his temple. It was towards the end of the interview that he sat back straight up, and said, 'Young man,' pausing as he looked into my eyes, 'I will give you a piece of advice that would do you good to remember all your professional life.'

'If you come to office on time; if you are diligent in your work; if you build excellent relationships with your peers and are respectful towards your seniors; if you meet your targets; if you work hard and smart and comply with the ethos of the company,' he paused as he added sonorously, 'Please note that you have done the bare minimum. It is what you do beyond is what will count for your growth.' I could feel the silence in the room as I took in the purport of his declamation.

It was a phenomenal piece of advice to have been privy to, at the start of a career, one that has stayed back with me over the years. I have since always questioned my own actions and intentions, striving to look beyond the ordinary, extending myself in areas that fell way out of my comfort zone.

My days in Madras were largely uneventful. I was tagged along with Soundar Rajan, a senior sales engineer, who acted as a peer-mentor and who I used to accompany on his sales calls to various kinds of businesses, picking up the finer nuances of the trade.

A tall and handsome south Indian Iyengar, Soundar was extremely sharp and witty and an absolute joy to be around with. Nothing in life seemed to faze him as he breezed in and out of customer calls, haranguing customers at the very mention of a competitor's name and breathing down the necks of docile accountants to collect dues. He readily took me under his wing and we hit it off mightily.

All sales engineers at Indian Oxygen were issued a Standard Herald car for their sales call, which was a luxury even in those days and bespoke of the clout Indian Oxygen held over the market. Soundar had a new model Standard Herald. A grey-coloured box with sharp lines, round headlamps and canine-like metal shock-absorbers tacked to a shiny steel bumper assembly, it took us across the length and breadth of our territory, and soon became a familiar sight to our customers.

Indian Oxygen gave me deep insights into the way factory workers plied their trade and the deep-seated British notion of class and hierarchy. The organisation worked as one gigantic piece of machinery, cogs and wheels of different sizes held firmly in place by resilient rules, policies and agreements.

I found the behaviour of factory workers perplexing and marvelled at how they differed from state to state. It was best brought to light in the case of gas regulator repairs.

As I was doing the rounds of the factory, trying to make the best of a particularly lazy day, I came across a large tool room at one end of the factory. The long rows of tables were occupied by workers in various stages of disassembling a variety of gas regulators. Curiosity got the better of me as I stepped into the room to have a closer look at the workmen hunched over the regulators as I chatted with their supervisor.

A majority of gas regulators then were driven by basic mechanics; the meters would have either two or more chambers formed by moveable diaphragms or two rotors spinning in precise alignment, regulating the flow of gases. The system also housed a mechanism to display a speedometer-like needle mechanism to indicate the pressure of gas in the cylinder. These meters were often prone to malfunction with either the needle coming off or the diaphragms losing their alignment. Given the large sales volume, it became a practice for customers to order for extra regulators with each order of gas cylinders—and equally copious quantities of defective regulators came through the doors of the regional factories for repairs.

According to the supervisor, this onerous workload necessitated the management to reach an agreement with the workers to ensure that a fixed number of such defective regulators were repaired on a daily basis and despatched to the regional offices for onward delivery to their clients. The agreement also included a healthy incentive scheme for each additional regulator fixed by a worker. The idea was thrashed about and finally, an amicable agreement was arrived at with the national workers' union. The agreement was duly executed, across all factory locations, with the daily quota of defective regulators to be fixed remaining constant across states.

The supervisor was proud of his team, especially for the commitment to meeting the target numbers and invited me to swing by their shed in the evening to witness that for myself.

As I entered the shed that evening, the end-of-shift hooter blared out, as if heralding my visit. The workers took off from their work benches and queued up to wash their hands before heading across to the row upon row of lockers to change out of their work uniforms. A highly disciplined lot, they then piled into the buses that were lined up to cart them to various points in the city.

The supervisor showed me the tally, which met the day's repair target. He was duly proud and reeled off the weekly repair numbers with aplomb.

As I invited the supervisor for a cup of tea at our hall, my mind swung back to what I had noticed at the Calcutta factory during my training days.

Being a larger operation, the guys at the Calcutta factory had a whole repair section to themselves. Here, an entirely different routine ensued. Workers would be done with repairing their daily quota of regulators by 3 p.m. Each did a meticulous job with hardly any complaints from any quarter.

A wash later, some of the workers would conjure a variety of electric heaters to magically appear from various nooks and crannies and get busy drumming up spicy omelettes, which were then sandwiched between two slices of bread. Some of their brethren, in the meantime, would spread out large reed mats and keep a large kettle of hot bubbling tea at hand.

Appetites whetted and buoyed by the hot tea, they would sit in circular groups and launch into a variety of card games. This they did until the end-of-shift hooter sounded, the more passionate ones tarrying behind to complete the game at hand.

No manner of sweet talking or coaxing could get them to repair a single additional regulator beyond their daily quota. They had discovered the value of 'me time' much before the world had woken up to the fact. This nonchalant attitude towards monetary gain and larger productivity-driven issues was lost to their sense of idealism. This perhaps gave Bengal its finest laureates and also its fiercest anarchists.

It was also during my stint at Indian Oxygen that I often dwelled on how Indians came about with the dubious distinction of being subservient to their rigid caste system, while the British had developed theirs to a fine art—right down to the table mat!

Though we had done away with the last vestiges of British rule, it had left in its wake a slew of companies that steadfastly hung on to the colonial practices of the past. This legacy was nowhere more profound than at Indian Oxygen, brought to the fore during tea service.

Junior officers like us were offered tea at our tables in matching cups and saucers. Personnel lower down the ranks, comprising mostly factory workers and supervisors, weren't deemed fit for such largesse and had to stand in queues, cups in hand, for tea to be served from a large dispenser with a brass tap welded at the bottom that spewed tea in angry bursts.

Senior officers and above were deprived of tea and were served coffee instead—and had their coffee served in dainty little trays! The higher up the hierarchy you went, the bigger the tray got, till it reached a point where the tray came bedecked with a 'pukka' tea service, tea cosy et al. What if a junior officer yearned for coffee or a senior officer for some tea for a change? The carefully crafted class system ensured that the tea–coffee imbroglio could never be bridged!

◆

It was soon time to bid goodbye to Madras and I was glad to do so. I had started getting weary of following the banal routine of tagging along with Soundar on his calls, reporting back to the factory at the end of the day and spending largely solitary evenings by myself. Some days, I took a bus down to the local Bengali association centre, but the meagre population and the dearth of young men of my age failed to assuage my feelings of boredom and loneliness.

I yearned for some action interspersed with long-drawn *adda* sessions over piping hot samosas and tea, but there were none to be.

Eight

It was a pleasant friday afternoon of January 1975 when I got off at the Vizag station, or more appropriately, almost didn't get off!

As the train chugged in into the latest station, I read the large yellow board—customarily positioned at the peripheral ends of the platform—announcing the current halt as Waltair Junction. I stayed put in my seat before an elderly gentleman, whom I had befriended on the way, prodded my arm and asked me, 'I thought you said you were getting off at Vizag, young man?' 'Yes,' I said, happily adding, 'but we haven't arrived at Vizag station, have we?'

'Young man,' said the gentleman, thrusting my copy of the day's newspaper in my hands, 'the train has halted at Vizag station and will take off in the next three minutes if you don't hurry.' How was I to know that the customary yellow board wouldn't have Vizag or Visakhapatnam written on it and instead scream Waltair Junction!

I bundled out of the train in a rush, shoving my luggage before me as I waved a hurried goodbye to the kind gentleman. It was a close shave as I planted myself on the platform in the nick of time as the train blared its horn and started rolling down the platform, thankfully without me still on board.

As I checked into my hotel and settled in, I suddenly felt very lonely. True, I had got used to living independently since my IIT days, but it was also for the first time that I was truly alone with no one around for help or advice. I fell back upon what I did best—draw up meticulously detailed plans to chart my next course of action.

I spread out the tortuously folded city map of Vizag, covering almost the whole breadth of the hotel bed, lit a cigarette, and busied myself for the next hour, crouched over the paper city, locating in that order, my office, movie theatres, eateries and finally, a suitable residential neighbourhood to rent myself a perch in.

By the time I was done, I had managed to fill in two pristine pages with a heavily renumbered list of action items ranging from 'Saturday Morning: Get a haircut' to 'Sunday Afternoon/Evening: Look up office building and recce Seethammadhara area for a suitable tenement'.

It was much later that I regretted not having a decent-sized kitchen as part of my one-room apartment as I had merrily planned on eating out, which apart from draining my stretched finances had a telling effect on my health.

Indian Oxygen's Vizag division was small compared to both the Madras and Calcutta operations. The office, housed in a single-storeyed residential building in Seethammadhara, was close to the factory; the entire operation was helmed by the area sales manager, Mr V. Balagopalan, my first boss, and Mr R.S. Sharma, the factory manager. Between them, they ensured a healthy revenue run rate and a batch of happy customers.

Vizag then had none of the hustle and bustle of a big metro. Life moved slowly. I spent the first few weeks getting briefed on the market and familiarising myself with the widely dispersed network of distributors and dealers. We rarely dealt directly with end-customers, except for large corporations, the real bulk-users of our various products.

Mr Balagopalan, my boss, was also new to Vizag. A blue-eyed boy of the management at Indian Oxygen, he had been recently promoted as an area sales manager and given independent charge of the Vizag territory. It was extremely rare those days for young officers in their mid-30s to be promoted so early in their careers or to be given a free rein. Age and length of service were the defining benchmarks when it came to progressing up the corporate ladder.

Mr Balagopalan turned out to be unlike any of the senior officers that I had encountered earlier, both during my training days at Calcutta and the short internship at Madras.

Hailing from an extremely well-bred south Indian Brahmin family, he had an aversion to the strict formality and rigidness of hierarchy, which was the norm of the day. Extremely clear on our individual roles, he viewed relationships horizontally (as opposed to vertically, which was the norm) and believed in giving his people both freedom and space to discover their talent. To him, I was 'the' technical person and fully trusted me in my judgement, never for once treading into my turf.

∽

Nine

Early on in my career at Indian Oxygen at Vizag, Mr Balagopalan stopped by my table, one regular work day morning, with a request to travel to Bailadila, an iron ore-rich region of Andhra Pradesh, now part of Chhattisgarh, to help conduct a study on how Indian Oxygen could help the state-run National Mineral Development Corporation (NMDC) ensure that its mining equipment was more wear-resistant.

It was my maiden visit to India's first large-scale open-cast mechanised iron ore mine and the humungous expanse of the operational area took my breath away. Commissioned in April 1968, the Bailadila iron ore range extended for a length of 40 km with a width of about 10 km, running along the top of the hill and constituted one of the richest concentration of iron in the world at 66 per cent iron content, free from sulphur and other deleterious material.

As I was taken around the activity areas of Bailadila—14 open-cast mines—by a senior project executive, I marvelled at the gigantic mechanised shovels as they tore through the surface of the earth, coming up with huge loads of rocks laden with ore. The NMDC official went on to explain how the teeth of the shovels were prone to breaking free from the main bucket after a few uses owing to the hardness of the surrounding surface rocks and the hard lumpy ore.

Back in Vizag, I reported my findings to Mr Balagopalan, who by the end of the meeting, requested me to conduct a detailed research on the subject and submit a comprehensive report detailing my findings and possible solutions to the problem vexing the NMDC officials.

'Take no more than 10 days on it, Bikram, the earlier the better…this has to go to HQ,' he said, winking at me, before he disappeared into his cabin. Mr Balagopalan always winked. It was his way of leaving things unsaid.

With no Google at hand, I spent the next few days burying myself in books and trade and technical magazines, anything that I could lay my hands on, until I was convinced enough that I had achieved some degree of command over my subject.

The solution, to my mind, lay in a special technique called 'hardfacing'. 'Hardfacing' was a metalworking process where harder or tougher material was welded to the base material. 'Hardfacing' by arc welding was the typical surfacing operation in use to help extend the service life of industrial components.

'Hardfacing' could be applied to a new part during production to increase its wear-resistance or it could be used to restore a worn-down surface. This I deduced would result in significant savings to NMDC from having lower machine downtime and also cutting down on production costs.

In the meantime, as luck would have it, I had a bad fall from a bike and was unable to move about freely, let alone attend office. I was put up by a kind friend and Mr Balagopalan made it a point to send across his car every morning and evening to ferry me to and fro from office. It came naturally to Mr Balagopalan to do so—an act that broke away from the tight bonds of hierarchy maintained at Indian Oxygen those days.

Somewhat satisfied that I had hit upon the right solution, I dived into writing the report with a great deal of pride, rattling away at the typewriter, preferring to type out the report myself, instead of handing it over to one of the many steno typists that abounded. I made it a point to make the report as exhaustive and self-explanatory as possible, lacing it with hand-drawn drawings to explain the finer nuances of the 'hardfacing' technique, while detailing the kind of welding to be used replete with gases, electrodes et al.

I agonised over the report, re-reading and revising it countless times, all the while dreading that I would miss the deadline. It was late into the night on the ninth day that I was somewhat satisfied with the outcome, confident that I had covered all the major issues that needed to be dealt with.

I handed over the report to Mr Balagopalan the next morning with a great deal of trepidation. 'Sit, Bikram, sit,' he commanded, as he proceeded to go over the report, occasionally nodding his head, as he lifted his gaze from the paper and looked at me.

He winked at me as he put the report down and proceeded to write a brief covering note. 'Dear Sir', he wrote, in his extremely stylish hand, addressing a personal note to the managing director of Indian Oxygen, 'Please find enclosed, as desired, the report on Bailadila Open Mine Iron Ore Project, by Bikram Dasgupta', before signing off with the customary salutations.

I felt extremely proud and humbled as I stepped out of Mr Balagopalan's chamber that morning. The incident had a profound impact upon my young mind. I saw the value of giving a person his due and the finer nuances that went into building a team of committed soldiers.

I had learned my first of many invaluable lessons in management and people-handling skills and recognised how important it was for youngsters to have a 'Balagopalan' in their lives as their first boss.

◆

I finally landed myself a suitable dwelling in the vicinity of my office after a week of searching; being particular about what I needed, I would send out the local Telugu peons on countless exploratory trips—disrupting many a landlord's peaceful afternoon siesta.

Located next to a small park and at the end of a long lane, it was a stand-alone one-room house seemingly purpose built for letting out. Part of a larger residential building, the dwelling had its own little patch of garden, no larger than a handkerchief, and an independent access away from the main house. I could choose to come and go as I pleased.

I liked it as soon as I had laid my eyes on it and patted the peon for his discovery, pressing a ₹5 *baksheesh* into his palm. Owned by a retired Telugu couple, they seemed happy to have a young man in their midst, their own children having migrated to different parts of this vast country.

The monthly rental was a different matter altogether. I had to shell out more than what I had bargained for—all for the sake of independence and a patch of earth. I didn't mind that. I never did. When it came to money, I always found myself spending more than

I planned. 'Saving' was a word alien to me for a large part of my life.

I shifted to my new abode that same evening. It was a delightful room with a pair of large windows on the eastern side, which overlooked my little patch of earth. As you entered, you turned left to enter the small kitchen, with its neat stone countertop and an array of symmetrically stacked shelves lining the walls. I smiled at the thought of Ma looking approvingly at the set-up.

Dinner, however, posed a formidable challenge. The nearest eatery was some 2 km down the road and one had to invariably walk the distance. Rickshaws were sporadic as most people owned two-wheelers, the preferred mode of transport during my time at Vizag.

I was winded by the time I returned. I unrolled the holdall and retrieved the thick mattress, spreading it near the window. I spent the first night sleeping on the floor; sleep was hard to come by with mosquitoes landing on every bit of exposed skin that they happened to spot. I finally fell into an exhaustion-driven sleep, counting the dimples on the ceiling.

Mr Balagopalan understood my predicament when I met him the next day. He gave me a half-day off, handed the keys to the office Willys Jeep, and a peon to help me navigate through the tedious haggling process.

The aid of the local Telugu peon was a godsend as we went around some of the busiest markets in Vizag, hopping from store to store, till I had satisfied myself that I had got the basic creature comforts, which included a bed, a pair of neat foldable wooden chairs, a compact study table and an assortment of kitchenware with an electric heater leading the pack. Not for me the tediousness of lighting a kerosene stove. Gas was not widely used back then, with the waiting period stretching across years.

The 1970s were when socialists ruled from coast to coast. Politicians and bureaucrats alike were enamoured with the Soviet model of Five-Year Plans, which they implemented with gusto. The government went into the business of running businesses, owning banks, airlines, petroleum and heavy industries. Red tape throttled the growth of businesses and enterprises. Common necessities like cooking gas and a telephone connection were treated as luxuries, to be flaunted by the few families who had access to these.

As I settled into life at Indian Oxygen, I frequently found myself with the old Willys on the road on calls to various distributors and dealers across the city. Most of my calls were technical, more in the way of advising dealers on the best uses of our products and ensuring safe work practices. Industrial safety practices were hardly followed and many workers came within an inch of their lives carelessly handling extremely inflammable gases.

I was accorded a warm welcome wherever I went. It was prestigious to be an Indian Oxygen dealer and people generally vied for your attention. I enjoyed the attention and feting, but soon got tired of it. I sometimes cringed at all the attention—it felt false—making me feel like a pretentious brat.

I loved doing the rounds in the city and its outskirts, driving down its winding roads, the tarpaulin top of the Willys flapping wildly in the breeze. The Willys, I suspected, was a well-maintained old army issue. The ageing diesel engine would start with an unmistakeable shudder, as if woken from a deep slumber, before setting itself to a 'rev' that made it growl like a big cat.

Life moved at a steady, unhurried pace. I was never the kind of person to sit around the office pushing paper, preferring instead to be out in the sun, doing the rounds of my dealer's offices. Mr Balagopalan, too, enjoyed the outdoors and the pair of us often found ourselves on the road for the better part of a month.

Mr Balagopalan had a sharp eye for business and people. He keenly observed me during my calls. He did so unobtrusively, trusting in the instincts of his executives to pull through a call. I can't recollect a single instance where he interjected me in the middle of my pitch, even if I happened to step off the rails at times. He would use his charm and uncanny ability to crisply summarise a call, neatly glossing over the areas that I happened to totter over.

Feedback sessions were invariably held the next day. He preferred to have me mull over the day's calls before dispensing any advice. He hated pontificating and never ran you down.

As Mr Balagopalan's confidence grew, he started entrusting me with more responsibilities, and I soon found myself independently handling marketing and sales assignments for select territories and large accounts.

Rajahmundry happened to be one such territory. Situated some 190-odd km from Vizag, on the banks of the mighty Godavari—the second longest river in India after the Ganga—Rajahmundry was among the major cities in Andhra Pradesh and a rapidly growing commercial hub.

One morning, as I sat at my desk, clearing some odd papers that had piled up, I received a call from the office of one of our larger distributors in Rajahmundry. The owner-manager was en route to Vizag on a business trip and requested me to spare a couple of hours for a meeting.

The gentleman, drapered in a well-appointed suit, arrived by noon. Having dispensed with the usual pleasantries, I soon realised that the sole reason for the four-and-a-half hour drive down was to meet the young man now in charge of his territory.

I took the gentleman around to our factory, a couple of blocks from our office, and gave him a rundown of our facilities. I introduced him to Mr Sharma, our factory manager, who, in the absence a regular audience, gladly launched into all matter of production-driven talk, showing off his latest machines and reeling off production numbers, before I rescued my man and whisked him away for lunch at one of the more fancy joints at Palm Beach Hotel.

We discussed business and I piled on my man to increase his order book, citing the growing clout of Rajahmundry as a commercial hub. He hemmed and hawed his way through my pitch, at times furiously nodding his head as if in righteous agreement. The south Indian nod is a difficult one to decipher—something that I had caught early on during my days in Madras.

As we stepped out into the warm sunlit parking lot, the gentleman took my hand and escorted me to his car—a brightly coloured Ambassador—saying, 'I have a small gift for you, Mr Dasgupta.'

I in my naivety, felt gratified and expected a small token knick-knack. The gentleman tapped on the car window and a driver sprung out from the car and held the passenger door wide open. I spied a mint new black briefcase lying on the seat.

'Here, Mr Dasgupta, here is your gift,' our man said, pointing at the briefcase.

'What is it?' I asked, glancing away from the briefcase to look my man in the eye.

'Ah! Mr Dasgupta, go on, open the briefcase. I am sure you will like it.'

I reached for the briefcase and gingerly unsnapped its lock. One glance and I slammed the lid shut. It was full of cash—wads of ₹100 bills—neatly stacked and arranged.

I was dumbstruck. Was this man, so genial and well-spoken, trying to bribe me? I felt a stream of anger welling up inside me.

'What is this?' I shouted. 'You can't do this to me…what do you take me for?' I was almost hysterical by now.

The man stepped back from the car and firmly shut the door. He was taken aback, not expecting this reaction—least of all my raw hysteria.

'It's fine, Mr Dasgupta…don't worry…forget about this…forget that this ever happened,' he said, trying to sooth my frayed nerves.

But I was not to be soothed. I took off, ignoring his outstretched hand. I started the Willys and thundered down the road.

The incident unnerved me and I couldn't shake it off. I couldn't fathom why the man would have wanted to bribe me. Was it something in my demeanour? Did I lead him on in some way? I asked myself. Perhaps he wanted some favours done. But what kind of favours? Perhaps he wanted an inside man at Indian Oxygen, I told myself. It was all a bewildering mess for a twenty-four-year-old.

As I lay down that night, I recalled how furious Baba would get if someone tried to push him up the wrong path, something that he deemed unethical and against the rule book. He would fume for days, keeping up a constant tirade, ruing how the corrupt were destroying the very fabric of society.

Baba was a stickler for honesty and never shied away from standing up to his bosses. He raved and ranted at the smallest of injustices. But the system did not appreciate an honest bureaucrat and he ended up getting transferred some eight or nine times in his long career. Baba took it in his stride and made it a point to say, 'But look, I can sleep peacefully for seven hours each night.'

Ten

BEING A RELATIVELY SMALL TERRITORY, work pressure wasn't demanding and I found myself free by early evening. As I settled down, the evenings became even lonelier and the nights longer.

One evening, as I sat pondering if I should catch a movie, it struck me that there might be a Bengali association in Vizag. 'There isn't a place on earth where you wouldn't bump into at least one Bengali...' Ma used to say with a laugh. Her other jokes were far unkinder.

Not wishing to tarry any longer, I knocked at my landlord's door. The petite old lady of the house welcomed me with a beaming smile, made sure I was comfortable in her tastefully done sitting room, and went to fetch her husband. The lady spoke in broken English and knew not a word of Hindi.

Mr B.R.P. Kalluri was a man of the world. A central government servant, he had served in a number of state capitals with a short three-year stint in Calcutta thrown in. He had zoomed in on Vizag, having visited the city a number of times on official errands, as his preferred retirement destination and had built this old-age perch some two years before he was due to be relieved.

'There is a sizeable Bengali population in Vizag,' he said in response to my question.

I detected a fair hint of pride in what he said. Vizag was a cosmopolitan city.

'They have a Bengali association here too...it's somewhere on or near Thompson Street, I have been told,' he added.

'They conduct one of the biggest Durga Pujas here at Vizag at the Town Hall, in the One Town area, and I always make it a point to pay a visit during Asthami to offer my prayers.'

'In fact,' he said, sounding conspiratorial, as he leant over, 'the Puja Bhog is a big attraction. That's when I miss being in Calcutta the most.'

Mrs Kalluri, who had in the meantime busied herself in the kitchen, appeared with a tray of freshly made snacks and tall glasses of chilled lemonade.

'It has been a tiring day in office, *nā koduku*,' she said, as she laid the tray down carefully, mindful of the blocks of ice swimming dangerously close to the rim of the glasses.

'Please,' she said, pointing towards the food. She had run out of her limited English.

(A Telugu peon later told me that '*nā koduku*' had meant 'my son'. I was touched.)

I tucked into the food hungrily, as Mrs Kalluri looked on smiling, occasionally glancing disapprovingly at her husband as he, too, tucked into the fries with gusto. The man, I gathered, must have been told to keep off fried stuff.

As the evening shadows grew longer, the couple were reluctant to let go of me. Mr Kalluri insisted that I say over for dinner, saying, 'You wouldn't mind having dinner with an old couple, would you?'

'I would love to,' I said, not wanting to disappoint the couple.

Telugu dinners (and lunches), as I was to discover, were elaborate affairs, quite like a Bengali household, except that they had a far larger number of curries, dals and other accompaniments that went with the rice, albeit served in smaller portions.

Mrs Kalluri, quite like a Bengali matron, buzzed over me and her husband as we sailed through dinner, piling us with more food. I was always reticent to say no and found myself bursting at the seams by the time I managed to wrangle out of the clutches of the well-meaning matriarch.

'Young boys can't eat these days,' she complained to her husband in Telugu.

'You very thin. Must eat,' she part-advised, part-admonished me, as she pushed a jar of betelnut-based mouth freshener towards me.

I whistled through my regular routine the next morning. Yesterday's dinner was a welcome break from the evening monotony. It felt good to be indulged by the old couple and it felt like being home after a long time.

A 30-minute ride took me to Thompson Street that evening. As I looked at the old building, situated opposite the ITC office, I understood why I had missed it during my forays to Beach Road. The entire ground floor was taken up by a nondescript car repair garage with old Ambassadors and Premier Padminis in various stages of disassembly. With no visible signage and most windows on the first floor shuttered, it looked desolate and I felt that the building could have done well with a fresh coat of paint.

I navigated my way through the sick bed of cars and found myself at the bottom of a stairwell.

I strode up the stairs and lingered for a minute at the door, tidying my hair and patting the shirt down. Squinting as I entered the door, adjusting to the semi-darkness of what seemed to be a small hall, I saw a row of rooms on one end—one particularly noisy with the sound of human voices. That room, I decided, would be my first port of call.

As I entered, I saw a number of young men hanging about, some lounging on the chairs that were strewn haphazardly across the room. I walked up to the tallest of the gentlemen, one who had stood up at the entrance of the stranger.

I introduced myself to him. I was welcomed with a round of warm handshakes and was readily taken into their fold. I had finally found myself a group that I could hang out with.

The Bengali Association Club had been formed in 1928 by a handful of Bengalis who had migrated to the city. Over the years, as more itinerant Bengalis came to the city, the society's numbers swelled. It subsequently took on a more cosmopolitan character by opening its doors to members of other communities. The inner core, however, was always run by Bengalis.

As with most associations, the elders generally passed the baton of running the activities to youngsters, preferring to form a sort of an elders' committee to guide and mentor them while organising major events such as the annual Durga Puja, when all hands were needed on deck.

Snehamay Nag, the gentleman who I had walked up to and introduced myself, along with Biswanath Roy (he was a senior by many years and was called Biswanathda by all), Rathindranath Sinha and Ratan Kumar Pal brought up most of the active youngster brigade that busied itself with all cultural aspects of the club. I, too, joined the motley group, driven by my love of the arts, particularly theatre, films and other stage events.

No longer alone in the city, I became a regular at the club. All of us discovered a camaraderie bound by our endless youthful energy and the need to keep ourselves gainfully engaged.

As the days rolled by, a friendship that was to last a lifetime blossomed between me and Snehamay. He was affectionately nicknamed Naga by the group. We both loved theatre and perhaps that's what drew us closer.

In time, I also came close to Ratan Kumar Pal and between us, we went on to form the club's first Film Society, screening the best movies and hosting some of the celebrities who happened to visit Vizag. I remember us hosting Smita Patil, an extremely versatile actor during her days.

I would be at the club every evening. It became a routine for me to rush back home from office, take a quick shower and grab a sandwich on the way to the club. I would be back only late into the night, having had my dinner at any one of the many eateries that I happened to take a fancy to.

While Snehamay had his bachelor pad in the One Town area, which was nearer to the club, mine was at quite a distance. With buses running on erratic schedules, I found myself hailing an auto-rickshaw most of the time, leaving a gaping hole in my pocket.

Saving, as I might have mentioned, was something that did not come to me naturally, but I also hated having to stare at a near empty wallet by the end of the month. Rent, food and transport was where most of my money went, not counting the two packs of cigarettes that I smoked daily. The rope was burning fast and eating out didn't help my cause either.

Solve one problem at a time, I chided myself, and transport happened to figure at the top of the list.

I dashed off a letter to Baba the following month, requesting among other things a loan to buy a motorcycle. I had managed to painfully put away a small amount of money, hoping Baba would bridge the gap. Baba wrote back in a week, asking how much I wanted.

Given my penchant for buying the best of things, unmindful of the cost, I held myself back and endured the pain of not straying within the vicinity of a Yezdi showroom. I loved the Yezdi 250. Muscular in stance and build, it was a motorcycle every young man dreamed of those days, apart of course from the king of all motorcycles—the Royal Enfield with its unique heart-wrenching thud.

The only motorcycle that came within my limited budget was a Rajdoot 175. I decided to live with it; better than buying one of those horrid scooters, I consoled myself.

I put the deposit down on a Rajdoot 175 and waited for two weeks for the delivery to take place. On the appointed day, Snehamay accompanied me to the showroom and we took delivery of the motorcycle.

As with all Rajdoots of my period, mine too, came in black, with a square headlamp bordered with a shiny chrome strip and chrome wheels. The design didn't agree with me, its boxy lines accentuated by Snehamay's Yezdi parked next to it. Making a compromise didn't leave a good feeling.

I never liked making compromises and have carried this trait with me throughout my life. I have always held firmly to the belief that one loses a bit of oneself with each compromise that one makes. But I must also hasten to add that it does not mean going overboard with the material things in life. It has to do with one's inner beliefs and essential being.

∽

Eleven

With my transport issue sorted, our group spent the hot summer evenings away from the closed confines of the club, biking along Beach Road or choosing to spend entire evenings on any of Vizag's many pristine beaches.

The sea and chilled beer kept us alive as we waited for summer to give way to autumn, eagerly looking forward to the festive season to come upon us. That would be the busiest period of our lives as we organised plays, conducted pujas, held concerts, showcased films and generally lived and breathed art.

Planning for the season's Durga Puja was kicked off almost two months in advance from the date Goddess Durga was to undertake her voyage to earth, her premarital home in her mortal form, accompanied by her four children. With no two Durga Pujas falling on the same date—the dates being decided according to the Hindu lunar calendar—the conducting of every Durga Puja is an elaborate process, irrespective of the scale of the celebrations, calling for meticulous planning and execution.

I readily joined the year's steering committee of young volunteers tasked with conducting the Durga Puja. The steering committee, in turn, set up a smaller set of teams, each tasked with a separate function from running fund-raising campaigns, organising cultural events to helping conduct the actual puja; which in itself is a highly demanding ritualistic process following strict Vedic practices.

Our club became a hive of activities as we started planning in right earnest. Days passed by at a furious pace as the ten-day celebrations drew ever closer. We gave up our beach life for canvassing from door to door every evening, raising funds for the event.

We carved up our territory between various groups and hardly left a door unknocked. Unlike today, corporate sponsorships were unheard of, and the entire puja was funded by individual contributions from citizens, with people from business and trade generally contributing higher than an average household. Competition was fierce, with each group vying to outdo the other, bantering at each other mercilessly.

Each group prided itself on a couple of individuals who were naturals when it came to canvassing for funds. It was great fun witnessing them in action as they spun their magic, putting on their best manners and literally sweet talking the family elders to parting with more than they were prepared to. They could have been among the most charismatic of sales professionals if they chose to, but most held sedate armchair jobs.

Mahalaya marked the first day of the ten-day festivities and has always held a special attraction, pulling at the heartstrings of every Bengali. I have not come across a single Bengali, from any quarter of the globe, who has not been stirred by the soaring voice of Birendra Krishna Bhadra reciting *Mahishashura Mardini*, a collection of Sanskrit shlokas and Bengali songs, celebrating the epic battle between Ashura Mahishashura and Goddess Devi Durga—an epic battle between good and evil.

Produced by All India Radio (AIR) way back in 1931, the script was written by Bani Kumar and set to music by the famous maestro Pankaj Kumar Mullick. The programme was a runaway success. The magic of Bhadra's voice has refused to die over the years, even though AIR made an attempt in 1976 to recreate the magic by using the voice of Uttam Kumar, the unparalleled doyen of Bengali cinema.

My earliest memories are of Ma waking up me and Dadamoni at around 4 a.m., whispering in an urgency that had a certain mystical quality about it, 'Wake up, it's Mahalaya today...the programme is about to begin.'

We sat huddled around Baba's Philips tube radio set as he fiddled with the knobs, scanning the airwaves, trying to lock onto AIR's Calcutta service at its clearest frequency.

Baba usually reclined in his lounge chair, arms folded behind his head and his eyes closed. He maintained this meditative posture all through the two-hour-long programme. I sat with Ma, at times resting my head on her lap, drifting between wakefulness and sleep as Bhadra's voice seemed to fill and reverberate across the room, creating an atmosphere that refuses to be captured in words.

Each year, Bhadra's *Mahishashura Mardini* revealed itself more and more to me as I understood the purport of the words and verses. As I grew up I used to listen, transfixed, getting goosebumps as Bhadra incanted, '*Ya Devi Sarvabhuteshu Vishnu-Mayeti Sadbita. Namastasyai, Namastasyai, Namastasyai Namonamah. Ya Devi Sarvabhuteshu Shakti-rupena Samsthita. Namastasyai, Namastasyai, Namastasyai Namonamah...*' in his rich baritone, the cadence unbelievably magical. We were, it felt, suffused with spiritual energy.

The Bengali Association Club's Durga Puja was itself rich in history. The oldest Durga Puja in Vizag, the first Sarbojanin or community puja was held during the pre-independence era in 1941 and the tradition has continued since. In 1953, the puja was moved to Vizag's iconic Victoria Memorial Town Hall and has been the puja's permanent venue till late.

With Mahalaya over, we had but five days at hand before the real festivities and social celebrations began. The Town Hall came alive as we swarmed the place, making the final preparations for the puja. A thousand different things seemed needed done.

Some of us took over the task of decorating and decking up the place—fit for the Goddess to make this her abode. We chased up electricians to festoon vast strings of brightly coloured light bulbs all around the venue. We got carpenters and professional decorators to build temporary stages where cultural programmes would take place every evening.

Each day's cultural programmes were divided into morning and evening slots, the morning slots usually being reserved for children and women and comprised various competitions, including blowing of the auspicious conch shell. The evenings saw plays being staged by well-known theatre groups from Calcutta or even faraway Delhi. Late evening slots were reserved for showcasing the most happening Bengali movies, beamed on giant screens using two reel movie projectors.

Late evening movie slots gave young lovebirds the rare opportunity to lurk shyly among the shadows, holding hands, away from the gaze of their elders. Romance blossomed during the five days of festivities and many a lonely heart found themselves their soulmates for life.

Some evening slots were reserved for showcasing local talent, mainly an ensemble of song and dance routines meticulously conceptualised and produced after hours of dedicated practice. People took up such arts with a passion and dedication that one could only marvel at. The sedate housewife suddenly took on a new form, forgetting home and hearth for the sake of the impending performance, sweating over the minutest of details to ensure a near-flawless performance.

The puja was thrown open to the public from Sasthi as the trickling in of people started picking up pace. The main surge of visitors would take place from the seventh to ninth day. We formed volunteer patrols to help control and guide the swelling number of devotees and curious sightseers.

Bhog or cooked food offered to the deity would be an elaborate affair. We would have the lads from tent houses, which provided all manner of materials needed to host a puja or party, put up giant open-air kitchens fenced off on the sides by stout canvas sheets and temporarily roofed, using a mesh of bamboo rafters covered with thin sheets of tin. They would also bring along enormous *kadais*, gigantic metal spatulas—almost as tall as an average teenager—huge pots and pans and a myriad other things.

We would vie to hire the best cooks (Oriya cooks were in high demand) and sailed out in the wee hours of the morning to the wholesale market. We bought equally copious quantities of ghee, oil, rice, dal, a variety of masalas and fresh veggies for each of the days when Bhog would be served.

We were eco-conscious much before environmental sensitivity became a more universally accepted phenomenon. We shunned the use of plastics or metal and instead served food on washed banana leaves. Water was served in small earthen tumblers. Devotees partaking of the Bhog would, when they were done eating, neatly fold the used banana leaves and throw them into large bins. The earthen ware went into a separate bin.

The four days of rituals went by in a frenzy of activity. We hardly had any sleep. Not that it bothered any of us. We seemed to have been imbibed with a strange energy from within.

The day of Vijaya Dasami dawned bright. There wasn't a speck of cloud to be seen. The married ladies of the club and the neighbourhood gathered around Devi Durga, queuing up to bid their Goddess goodbye as she travelled back to her marital home. She was feted with sweets and sprinkled with sindoor as a symbol and protector of her marriage.

As afternoon gave way to evening, we loaded the Goddess and her four children on an open-sided truck, bedecked with chain upon chain of marigolds, leaving only a small porthole for the driver to prevent him from crashing into the frenzied crowd surrounding the truck.

The smell of incense and camphor filled the air; the drummers picked up the beat, leading a mass of young men dancing wildly in gay abandon, as we slowly wove our way down Beach Road towards Ramakrishna Beach.

It felt sad to let Mother go as we immersed the idol into the clear waters of the Bay of Bengal. She sank slowly till we lost sight of her. It seemed she too was reluctant to leave her earthly children behind. Some of the lads swore that they saw tears stream down the Devi's cheeks.

I have seen grown men moved to tears at the sight of the slowly sinking idol. Such is the power that spirituality holds over man.

◆

We felt exhausted at the end of the ten-day period. Our attendance at the club dropped dramatically as we all caught up with sleep and gave our aching bodies a much-deserved rest.

With the Dussera holidays over, we rejoined our offices and life began to fall back into its familiar pattern. Ma had, in the meantime, decided to come and live with me for a couple of months.

With my elder brother, Dadamoni, married to a lively homely lady, Ma could safely leave Baba under her care and travel halfway across the country to live with me.

I met her at the platform on the appointed date; the train and coach number relayed ahead by Baba as soon as the train had left Howrah station. I felt good inviting Ma to my abode, done up independently and, I hoped, in good taste.

As I had suspected, she soon made a beeline for the small kitchen on the left and minutely observed its setting. She didn't quite like the electric heater, though the rest of the wares passed her muster. The maid had kept the kitchen neatly organised before she had taken off for the day.

I had made a separate bed for Ma and gave her the brightest spot in the room, next to the large windows, overlooking the small garden, somewhat weedy now since I found no time for gardening; it was something that I found no interest in.

With Ma taking over the household, I started eating healthy again. I had been beset with all manner of stomach ailments and had lost some weight. I didn't feel the loss weigh on me in any way, but then a mother always finds their children to be famished during their long absence from home.

Ma was not the one to chide or fawn over me. Her only lament was, when she laid her eyes on me at the railway platform, 'So, you have held on your reedy IIT looks, I see.'

I had something to look forward to in the evenings, not that I stopped frequenting the club. I would make it a point to be back from work on time to spend the first hour of the evening with Ma. I would leave her, sitting by the window on one of the folding wooden chairs, reading by the light of the low-hanging incandescent bulb.

She would get up when the clock chimed eight, neatly resting the book on the small reading table by the wall. She busied herself over the next hour-and-a-half, drumming up dinner for the two of us and making preparations for the next day's breakfast. She always ensured that I had a heavy breakfast while she was around.

She would then get back to her book and read till I reached home. She made it a point of us having dinner together, no matter how late it was.

Twelve

Life at the club fell into its regular routine. We were well into autumn and looked forward to the mild winter months ahead of us. It was during this period that the dramatics society at the club sprung to life. Snehamay led the charge and we passionately debated the first of the many plays that we were to stage that season.

We finally arrived at the final list of the four plays that we would stage that season. Snehamay was to direct them all. We would kick off the season with Bidhayak Bhattacharya's *Tahar Namti Ranjana* and end the season with Manoj Mitra's *Sajano Bagan* or more popularly identified as *Bancharamer Bagan*—a comic fantasy story. I was to figure in all of the plays and readily acceded to be cast as the lead character in the first and last of the plays.

We might have been amateurs, with none of us involved in commercially staging plays, but that did not dull our enthusiasm one bit. We produced and staged plays with a seriousness and dedication that would have rivalled professional theatre groups.

Tahar Namti Ranjana was a challenging play to produce and stage. The storyline had several layers, each intertwined into the other, suffused with emotion; at the surface, it was a simple story—a murder convict on his death row and his struggle in attempting to hide his actual identity when confronted by his younger sibling, a sister, in the final hour of his life.

Delve deeper and you observe an idealistic man who struggled against an unfair world and his struggle to earn a decent, respectable living. Delving still deeper, you would be confronted by a young man from an idyllic Bengal village, deeply in love with poetry and Poet Laureate Rabindranath Tagore, driven to desperation (and desperate acts) by the world that has lost all sense of propriety and takes it upon himself to deliver justice; in the process, losing his very soul and identity—no longer a simple village waif but a murderer in the eyes of law and society— someone to be reviled.

Between the team, we had decided that the script and stage setting were going to be the most challenging aspects in staging this complex play. With only four characters apart from the main protagonist—Kaushik, the man destined for the gallows; the success of the play would lie in a well-written script, creating the dark mood that enveloped the play and tight dialogue delivery.

Snehamay and I struggled over the script for weeks on end. We debated and discussed the minutest of details. I was always a stickler for details and wouldn't rest till we had ironed out the smallest of creases. It took three weeks before the entire cast was finally satisfied with the script and we embarked upon a rigorous rehearsal schedule.

We were all charting new territory with *Tahar Namti Ranjana*. While theatre and debating came easily to me, prodded on by Baba from early on in my childhood, I had never enacted such an intense character, one that called for a combination of acting and recitation skills—the title of the play itself being taken from one of Tagore's vast anthology of poems.

Those in our team who had experience with stage setting and lighting found themselves with a challenge at hand. Led by Snehamay, the director, they needed to come up with a stage design that resonated with the mood of the play. To add to their woes, the scenery itself was laden with symbolism and set well into the late hours of a full-moon night. If that weren't enough, the storyline kept moving back and forth in time with the lead character sometimes reminiscing about his past and at times, 'flash forwarding' as it were, imagining future events.

With the storyline moving rapidly back and forth in time, particularly in the second act of the play (we had divided the story into a two-act play), we decided that it would be near impossible to reset the stage at such short intervals and instead started looking at a number of radically different approaches—those that none of us had tried before.

As we grappled with the problem, Snehamay came up with what seemed an impossible idea—shadow play. None of us had any experience with shadow play technique, although we had seen some form of shadow play at travelling circuses and fairs, which were a rage back then in India.

Shadow play has a rich history in India and was a popular storytelling technique, using a variety of articulated figures or shadow puppets. Most of the stories were centred on folktales and epics, such as the Ramayana and Mahabharata. In fact, records of *Tholu Bomalatta*, the ancient shadow play technique popular in Andhra Pradesh, have been found dating back to 200 BCE.

Most of us felt trepidation using the shadow play technique, albeit with live actors instead of puppets, but Snehamay's conviction and unbridled enthusiasm won us over. However, one challenge remained.

We couldn't try out our shadow play idea in full till the day earmarked for the dress rehearsal since we didn't have enough funds to recreate the stage with all the lights that we wanted to help create the perfect shadow effect.

Rehearsals were strenuous but great fun. I have a hazy recollection of the lady who played Kaushik's sister, but her name fails me. What struck me was her vivaciousness and willingness to slog it out with us. She was a good actor with an erudite Bengali diction and a voice that had a singsong quality about it. Her voice carried the deep filial emotion of Ranjana—the character that she was playing—so well that the character seemed to come to life. We gelled well and rarely summoned the aid of a prompter to help with the lines.

Little did I know that in some years a Ranjana was to figure again in my life in a big way!

We were so engrossed in our rehearsals that we were scarcely aware of the passing days and soon found ourselves perilously close to D-Day.

We hauled ourselves to the Town Hall for two evenings of full dress rehearsals. We lost almost the whole of the first evening setting up the stage. With rudimentary automation available for controlling and sequencing the lighting arrangements, we had to resort to a series of trial and errors before we could get all the lights correctly installed and wired to a central console.

The large scrim, on which the shadow would be cast, was suspended between the downstage and apron area; we installed a series of pulleys and levers to suspend and fold the scrim, as the need occurred, and which could be controlled from either of the wings.

The day of the play's opening arrived and all of us were taut with a fair degree of stage fright. I have always inwardly maintained that a certain degree of stage fright, irrespective of the number of stage appearances one made, does wonders to the final performance. I have carried this trait over with me to the professional business world where I would endlessly rehearse my presentations and pitches, till the last minute, always mindful of the pitfalls and an urge not to fail or falter.

Snehamay paced about the crossover area of the stage, checking and rechecking the final set-up when one of the lights strung up, to be shone on the characters to generate their shadow on the scrim, went out of alignment and the shadow appeared crudely distorted.

With 20 minutes to go before curtain-up and a rapidly filling hall, we were staring at disaster.

Snehamay pounded down the stairs and had four lads lug in a large ladder used by the in-house electrician. We had one of the spry lads quickly amble up the ladder as it swung in the air with six men holding on to its legs for dear life. We had the light adjusted with minutes to spare and all of us heaved a sigh of relief.

The play opened without any further disaster and all of us gave a performance that we were proud of. We had pulled off one of the most difficult plays of the season to near perfection.

As the cast and crew members stood with their hands folded, some bowing deeply, soaking in the adulation of the crowd, I suddenly found myself lost in reverie, transported back to my school days, when I was in standard eight or nine at Andrews School in Calcutta.

I had acted in the lead role of *Ankur*, directed by our Bengali teacher. This was a five-act play and every time the curtain went down, between the acts, I would hear an announcement in Bengali saying, 'Mr Tarakeswar Mukhopadhyay, moved by the performance of Shriman Bikram Dasgupta, proposes that a gold medal be bestowed on him.' I walked away that day clutching five gold medals and my first public adulation.

The audience gave us a thunderous ovation at curtain call and the play went on to enter the annals of fame during my years at Vizag. The play was the talk of the town for the season and somewhat eclipsed our other productions. I was feted by the Bengali population for my performance and in the process made new acquaintances within the sparse community.

∾

Thirteen

ONE OF MY MOST ENDURING FRIENDSHIPS during my days at Vizag that I carried forward in my later life came about serendipitously. With a bike and the office jeep available during working hours, I found it easier to traverse around town trying out various food joints. I found none suitable enough for regular patronage and hopped from one place to the next, never having more than two to three meals at the same joint.

I was on one of those hunts for an untried joint when I happened to chance across a curiously named restaurant with a chubby, happy-looking pink elephant as its mascot. The name Pink Elephant Bar and Restaurant tickled my imagination and I decided to give it a shot.

As I stepped into the nicely lit interiors, I was taken in by the profusion of red all over. The tables were round—topped with tastefully patterned red Formica laminate—instead of the regular rectangular tables with garishly designed tops. The chairs, too, were upholstered in a matching red fabric and one sank into the soft cushion. At the far end of the restaurant stood the bar with regular high stools, at the corner of which sat a young man apparently managing the till. The owner had evidently spent both time and money to spruce up the place nicely and it exuded the pride with which he ran the place.

'Seems to be a nice place…after a long time,' I congratulated myself as I occupied one of the round red tables and settled in.

As I ordered a bottle of beer and some snacks to munch along, my eyes fell on the pair of matchboxes placed along with a nice glass ashtray on the table. The matchbox had a picture of a colourful bird engrossed in a chat with a worm complete with a tagline saying, 'Where incredible friendships begin…'

I marvelled at this simple low-cost marketing ingenuity and tucked away the details which I was to use somewhat differently much later in my life.

As I sat nursing the chilled beer, I could see the head behind the bar pop up and down, at times rushing to the kitchen or greeting a familiar entrant with a friendly wave. It was not difficult to deduce that the bobbing head belonged to the owner of this nicely decked joint.

It was not long before the young man came across to my table and extending his hand said, 'Hi! I am Sohan Hatangadi,' to which I replied 'Bikram Dasgupta,' shaking his hands warmly.

I was struck by the youth and exuberance of the owner as he settled himself across me, saying, 'You seem to have an observant eye, Bikram! You wouldn't mind me calling you by your first name, I hope? Do you like what you see?'.

'I do. I really do. This is a nice place, better than all the joints that I have been to before,' I responded, before holding up the matchbox, saying, 'Brilliant!'

That evening, two complete strangers bonded over a couple of pints of beer—a serendipitous bond that lasts till today. The Pink Elephant Bar and Restaurant remained my go-to place for as long as I was in Vizag.

The Pink Elephant happened to be Sohan's first and solo jump into entrepreneurship and occupied most of his time starting from late afternoon and stretching well into the night. During the early hours of the day, he helped his dad, Mr Mohan Hatangadi, one of the pioneers of the refrigeration business in Vizag, run his contract engineering operations along with his elder brother Chandan.

The family had a way with names and called their engineering ops MOCHASO Engineering Co., every pair of letters picked from the first pair of letters that made their first names. Pronounced 'mochaso', the name was easy on the lips and had a nice ring to it.

These innocuous encounters and exposure to early attempts at innovative branding and marketing techniques must have impacted my young mind, subconsciously filing away the finer nuances of learning, which were to come to the fore during my later entrepreneurial years.

As I matured over the years, I have realised that learning can spring forth from the most mundane of incidents and experiences, however far apart they may have been from the rough and tumble of the entrepreneurial world. It does well to have an observant eye and a keen sense of listening with your ears as close to the ground as possible.

Sohan and I got along famously and he introduced me to the whole gang that he was close to, including Jayant Bayankar. We made quite a trio. Most of Sohan's enduring friendships came from the Pink Elephant, where we used to assemble during most of the evenings—that was if I was not at the Bengali Association, rehearsing for an upcoming play or hosting a celebrity from the Bombay film fraternity as part of our film society.

Living not too far away from Pink Elephant, Sohan's family occupied a two-storey building in Dwarka Nagar, the ground floor doubling up as the factory and office for MOCHASO Engineering and the first floor as the family's living quarters.

It was quite often that I found myself at Sohan's house during my breaks from work or on returning from a late evening call, tagging along with Sohan where we pitched our individual non-competing products to customers. I naturally had an upper hand in such calls since Indian Oxygen was a much larger operation, with only Advani Oerlikon Ltd as its local competitor and that too, for its range of welding equipment.

Sohan's mother, whom I called Nilima mashi (she was a Bengali with her roots in Calcutta), loved to cook and entertain and like most Bengali matriarchs used to get mightily irritated if a youngster were to leave her abode without partaking of either lunch or dinner.

A quite earthly soul, her life revolved around her family and she rarely flew off the handle, though she hid within her bosom an erudite romantic soul. Lakkhi mashi, her younger sister, was quite different. More boisterous and capable of putting on a show of theatrics, she, in her maiden days, thought nothing about donning a pair of boxing gloves, borrowed from her hapless nephews, and proceed to give them a sound walloping, all in good competitive spirit.

Nilima mashi was also quite a sport and would take a good deal of well-humoured bantering from her sons without flinching. One such incident remains forever etched in memory.

Sohan and I had come up with a plan to view the spectacle of a solar eclipse from the terrace of their two-storeyed house. As the hour drew closer, Sohan, Jayant and I followed by a couple of friends and Chandan, his elder brother, trooped up the stairs and stood on the terrace looking at the sun through pairs of welding glasses borrowed from the MOCHASO workshop. We had last spied Nilima mashi busy in the kitchen, her back to us, drumming something up for the bunch of hungry young men.

As we stood gazing at the magnificent natural phenomenon, Nilima mashi came bounding up the stairs and burst into the open all out of breath, worry writ large on her face, 'Shabdhan goh...rectum *jole jabe!*' she shouted, as we split into loud guffaws at her gaffe. She smiled sweetly as she realised, too late, what a slippery tongued 'retina' could do!

Among my fondest memories of Vizag are the times spent with Lakkhi mashi at her tastefully decorated one-room tenement that stood at the end of a somewhat steep incline. She had by then married Feroze Patel, an extremely handsome and gregarious gentleman nicknamed 'Mr Personality' by Sohan and his gang. An extremely lovable personality, he had committed to memory possibly the largest anthology of jokes and could fish out the most appropriate ones at any given context. He was also a fantastic cook and had, strangely enough, specialised in the art of cooking eggs in innumerable ways.

By the time I had met Lakkhi mashi, Feroze uncle had been transferred back to Bombay where he worked for a company specialising in building ship flooring. Lakkhi mashi chose to stay back in Vizag with her children Madhu and Joydeep, perhaps due to the large extended family support that she had here.

Just like her elder sister, Lakkhi mashi loved to cook and enjoyed having company during her meal times. Thus, it was often that I found myself at her house during lunch hour on my way back from a sales call to Hindustan Shipyard. I would park my jeep at the start of the incline and walk my way up to be welcomed by her warm smile. I felt as if I was at home and in the company of a kindred soul.

Our bond was perhaps bound by the commonality of language, our love for theatre, and that we were both undying romantics at heart. In her, I found company to discuss the various plays that I was either acting in or directing and we finally ended up jointly acting in a couple of plays.

I was at Lakkhi mashi's place one day when she suddenly asked me, 'Care for some dried fish?' (Shutki Maach, as it is called in Bengal, is a hot favourite, particularly for people from East Bengal—now Bangladesh—and is something of an acquired taste because of its pungent smell.)

'Ah, I don't fancy myself eating that,' I responded with a certain degree of distaste.

'I see you haven't had the privilege of tucking into a well-prepared Shutki Maach. Come by my house this Sunday and I will treat you to some real Shutki Maach and a bottle of beer. Then we shall see!' she said emphatically.

As much as I liked going to her place, I didn't quite like the idea, but didn't want to disappoint the lady either. That Sunday, I was treated to a heavenly dish of Shutki Maach. Flawlessly prepared, it had none of its pungency and came richly spiced, which went down well with the beer.

To Lakkhi mashi's credit, I can still recall the taste today, but it was the only time in my life that I had ever had Shutki Maach.

With her quarters in the One Town area, which also hosted the large Anglo-Indian community of Vizag, she was a favourite with the community, earning her the sobriquet 'Aunt Suzy'. She was adept at putting on the wavy Anglo-Indian accent and hollering out to a passing Anglo-Indian, 'Hello man! It is a bloody pleasure seeing you man, up along with the sun, you lucky bugger!' making it difficult for us to suppress the gigantic waves of laughter that welled up within us.

To us, the Vizagites, the name of Bikram Dasgupta is a sweet package of nostalgia. The days that have flitted by carry special memories infused with lasting and indelible imprints very close to our hearts.

In the early 1970s (1975, to be more accurate), after an arduous day at Indian Oxygen, a youngster could be seen guiding his Rajdoot from Seethammadhara towards the Bengali Association Club. His quest was to seek an ambience of cultural activities of which he felt starved after his departure from West Bengal, in general, and IIT KGP, in particular.

He was with me, Snehamay Nag, in his dramatic experiments as he was with Ratan Pal in his film society programmes, meeting the famous director Shyam Benegal and the then rising actress Smita Patil. He acted in a couple of plays at the Town Hall during Durga Puja celebrations, the most notable being Bidhayak Bhattacharya's *Tahar Namti Ranjana* under my direction.

After his marriage, his wife Ranjana capably complemented his role in the society of Visakhapatnam. She was (and we are sure, still is) a marvellous singer of Nazrul Geeti.

In those days, his dynamism and creative passion, though quite apparent, was not finding its much-needed fuel. The people around him hardly realised at that time what he was destined to achieve. It is quite natural that the confines of Indian Oxygen was not enough for him. He left Indian Oxygen and joined an enterprising entrepreneurial group of men that had formed HCL, in the capacity of the key market development manager. It was a very daring step to have left the secure beaten track of an established profession and taken a plunge into an unknown area of uncertain future. All the more so because the computer industry of India was but a fledgling one in those days. But what happened subsequently is now history, as they say, and the saga can be found all over the internet.

We fervently hope and wish him a wonderful, happy, ever-successful life with his loving family around him. He must rise to greater and greater heights of success so that coming to know of his achievements we may always exclaim with pleasure and pride, 'Yes, that is our Bikram!'

Snehamay Nag (Naga)
(Friend and fellow Vizagite)

Fourteen

As LIFE ROLLED ON BETWEEN the office, club and the Pink Elephant, the youth brigade found themselves staring at the rapidly approaching final month of 1976. With most of the major festivities over and Christmas looming large over the horizon, Sohan, Jayant and I hit upon a plan to bid adieu to 1976 and welcome 1977 in style—the likes of which had not been seen in Vizag before.

Crafted as an all-night party with staggered ticket prices, we had plans to ring in the New Year with a bang and had tucked deep into our hearts the hope of raking in some moolah as well. All for a good cause, we assured ourselves.

With a new project to occupy ourselves, we got down to planning for the event in right earnest. As with all projects, we took to this venture as if our very lives depended on its success and vowed over large pints of beer to not let ourselves and, more grandiosely, Vizag down.

By the time we were done with putting the plan to paper, we were saddled with an outsized number of tasks ranging from the mundane to hiring a suitable venue, preferably close to the beach, and roping in a couple of cult bands to entertain our guests.

We spent days on end traversing the expansive shoreline of Vizag hunting for a venue and finally zeroed in on Sea View Hotel. Owned and managed by a gentleman who went by the name of Subramaniam, it was among one of the lesser-frequented lodges those days, despite it being a beautiful piece of property with a sprawling sea-facing lawn.

Some sharp negotiations later, we were able to hire the entire premises from the morning of the 31st till the morning hours of the first day of the New Year. Mr Subramaniam turned out to be a devout soul and let us have our way as we drove down his prices with a characteristic mix of youthful aggression and supplication.

With the venue firmly pocketed, we spent a few harrowing weeks trying to get the Pink Elephant's bar licence extended to our venue at Sea View Hotel for a few hours. We ran hard into Upamanyu Chatterjee's *Mammaries of the Welfare State* and found ourselves filling out mile-long forms, sometimes in triplicate, running from one babudom temple to the next.

We christened our event 'Fireball '76' and used a streaky red-and-orange fireball plunging from the sky as our mnemonic for the event.

We pooled in our meagre resources and managed to do a fair bit of advertisement in the local dailies. We would wake up in the wee hours of the morning and head for the main station from where the day's newspapers and magazines were distributed and cajoled the paper boys to slide in our 'Fireball '76' flyers into the folds of the newspapers and magazines.

As the day of the event drew closer, we were drawing a blank in our efforts to identify a couple of well-known bands when Mr Das, a fellow Calcuttan and one of the smartest of the Pink Elephant's stewards, claimed to know a certain Bultan from Calcutta who ran a band called Bultan's Band and specialised in western music ranging from country to pop, rock and jazz.

Das believed that he could convince Bultan and his band to troop down to Vizag if only we could pay for Das's train fare to and fro from Calcutta. We wasted little time and dispatched the fellow with a wad of cash to bring the band to town.

By the morning of the 30th we were seriously worried since we hadn't heard the faintest of squeaks from Das who had been in Calcutta for a week.

As we sat huddled at the Pink Elephant, mulling how to navigate the choppy waters that we found ourselves in, a long-faced Das chose to make his entry. His face told us all as he described how, despite beseeching Bultan, swearing on his job and life, to travel to Vizag for the gig, he had been heartlessly turned down. It seemed he would break into tears if we persisted interrogating him further as he returned the money that we had given him to be put down as an advance to Bultan.

With disaster staring at our faces, we wasted little time in calling everyone that we knew, trying to get leads for some decent local bands in Vizag. We worked the phones endlessly, each time getting to hear the same banal message: 'Have you been sleeping guys? Our band has been booked for months in advance.'

We looked at each other, disappointment writ large on our faces, but vowed to work the lines till we dropped dead.

'Fireball '76' kicked off with a blast as the guests started streaming in by the droves from early evening. We found it a struggle to keep a check on the guests, while a few of our friends kept a tab on the tickets and passes that we had doled out.

Meanwhile, we had spied quite a few guys lurking around in the shadows trying to slip in and this kept us on our toes, mindful that there were quite a number of young girls in the crowd of invitees. With crates of liquor lying around, we didn't want any nasty fights to break out.

Jayant Bayankar was put in charge of the bar and had the keys to the room where we had stocked up our supply of liquor. He made it a point to identify to our set of minders people who seemed highly inebriated and we made sure that they enjoyed the evening without creating a fuss.

The band that we had roped in at the last hour turned out to be better than expected and had the crowds swaying with their music as the night grew longer.

The party was going fine when we heard the sound of a loud and angry argument coming from the entrance of the lawn. By the time we reached the spot, we came upon a bleeding Jayant staggering towards us.

As we sat Jayant down and patched up his bruised upper lip, he described to us what had transpired.

'I was returning from the washroom when I a spied a couple of burly guys sneak into our liquor store and by the time I managed to rush into the room, the fellows had laid their hands on a few bottles,' he said.

He smiled wryly as he continued, 'I managed to snatch the bottles from them and having chased them off the grounds, returned to my perch when one of the younger kids came rushing in saying that someone had come to meet me at the entrance of the lawn.'

As he spoke it appeared that the fellows who had sneaked into the liquor store were from the local boxing club and one of them had been hurt in the scuffle with Jayant over a bottle of liquor. Angered at the ferocity of Jayant's response, his mates had sneakily called out Jayant to the lawn entrance and had punched him in the face before roaring off into the night on their motorbikes.

Hot-blooded as we were, we swore to extract our revenge and decided to wait till the party whittled down before we made any moves. Meanwhile, news of our fracas reached Chandan, Sohan's elder brother who happened to be in town, and he along with Sumant Bayankar, Jayant's elder brother, decided to teach the goons a lesson. We vowed to extract blood for blood.

Now with the senior gang in tow, the team chose to make their move at around 1.30 a.m. Some six or seven of the team members piled into Vishnu's old Ambassador in search of the boys who had punched Jayant.

Sohan, ever mindful of the probable consequences of their hot-headed actions, kept me shielded from the ruckus and despite my protestations told me as he sat in the car, 'It wouldn't behove of an executive of a multinational firm to be involved in an ugly fistfight. You have a career in front of you...you would do better to stay put till we return,' and saying so jumped into the car and roared off into the dimly lit streets of Vizag.

The boys eventually chanced upon the boxer gang having a leisurely dinner at a shack near King George Hospital. After carefully reconnoitring the place, the boys pounced on them with gusto, catching the gang by surprise. Chandan and Sumant had between them a fearful pair of fists and gave the gang a sound walloping before bundling the guy who had punched Jayant into the cavernous Ambassador and took off in a cloud of dust.

They drove down to a particularly sheltered part of the beach and had the malefactor up against a wall as someone prodded Jayant to extract his revenge. Jayant, in his anger, let loose a fearful right hook, sending the poor fellow sprawling on the sand.

The boxer gang, back at the restaurant, had escaped with some minor bruises, but their egos had been massively dented.

Unable to lay their hands on any of their attackers, despite keeping a strict vigil on the streets, they approached the cops who bundled off Chandan and Sohan to jail. The poor fellows had to spend a night in custody before the elders stepped in and bailed them out. It took a while before things got sorted out amicably and the case fizzled itself out.

The next year round when we approached Sohan's dad seeking his permission to do a repeat of our successful 'Fireball '76', he smiled at us and said, 'You guys did Fireball, but it were my b****s that were on fire.'

The poor gentleman had to do a great deal of running around between the cops and the court before a compromise could be worked out and we didn't grudge him for turning us down so poetically.

Sadly, there wasn't to be any Fireball thereafter.

Fifteen

I HAD BEGUN NOTICING A SUBTLE change in the tone of Baba's letters over the past few months. Ma and Baba had been to Vizag a little over a month ago, helping me recoup from a bad case of amoebiasis, that had left me drained and weak. They had travelled back to Calcutta with a great deal of concern about my health.

Of course, he was interested in how I was and liked hearing in detail about all the plays and other creative stuff that I engaged myself in; I imagined that it gladdened his heart to know that I was not all staid science and work. I found him talking more about how it would be good if I settled down in life and the virtues of family life.

I figured that talk about getting me married and settling down was dominating the dinner table discussion lately. My hunch proved true when Ma, true to herself, broached the subject in her next letter, asking me if I had someone in my life that I would like them to meet.

I was always a romantic at heart, fairly good-looking, and had the gift of the gab. But not all die-hard romantics, somewhat contrary to popular belief, are lucky enough to chance upon a lady of their dreams and take things forward.

I had resigned myself on that quarter and fell back to the age-old and tested method of leaving the onerous task of choosing a suitable bride on my parents. My responsibilities were limited to giving my approval and being available for the wedding ceremony.

My parents quickly got down to the task, spreading the word among their network of relatives and well-wishers, and it was not before long that I heard back from Ma.

Meanwhile, on the other side of the country, my future mother-in-law had been diagnosed with a particularly virulent form of cancer and was given six to eight months to live by her team of doctors. A learned and stoic woman, she took the news in her stride, but pleaded and hankered with her husband to look for a suitable groom for the youngest daughter.

With her eldest daughter happily married off, she worried endlessly about how her husband would cope in her absence with a young daughter in tow. The youngest was barely in her early 20s and had just about graduated from college and was looking forward to continuing her studies while pursuing her love of traditional Indian classical music, having already passed the rigorous Sangeet Visharad examinations.

Her husband, however, held on firm to his belief that it was too early for his youngest to be married off. Not one to be easily dissuaded, my future mother-in-law quietly let word out in the vast grapevine of her relatives that they should forward leads on any suitable groom and that they should do so at the earliest possible opportunity.

Among the first few to respond to my future mother-in-law's fervent appeal was one of her many cousins, Noton, who used to frequent Vizag along with her husband Deepak, who was then Kusum Products Ltd's area sales manager for Andhra Pradesh.

I don't happen to recollect how we met for the first time, but we hit if off well. I shared a warm and friendly relationship with Noton, whom I found to be refreshingly different from the ladies of the day. She was gregarious and unafraid of speaking her mind.

Noton remains, till this day, one of my best friends of all times. She is perhaps among the handful of souls with whom I could truly open up and discuss just anything and I have forever felt blessed for having such a rare and dear friend in my life.

Unbeknownst to me, Noton wrote back to her sister, describing me in detail while endorsing my candidature as the prospective groom for her niece. She also ferreted out my parents' address, on what pretext I can't still recollect, which she duly included in her missive to her sister.

With her husband adamant in his stand, my future mother-in-law wrote a six-page letter addressed to my dad. It was unheard of those days for a lady to write to the father of a prospective groom, and so she couched it in a fashion that conveyed that she had been somewhat forced by circumstances to write directly, in contravention of the prevailing customs, since her husband, unfortunately, was away on a long tour. This was the only instance that I ever heard of my future mother-in-law not being fully forthright with facts. She was to pass away some seven months after she had written that letter, depriving me of the opportunity of meeting her before my wedding—something that I still rue today.

My mother-in-law wrote extremely well and it struck a chord with my parents. My father because of his literary bent of mind and my mother due to her downright practicality. In her letter, as she described her daughter, she wrote with a rare conviction. 'My daughter, you must note,' she wrote in Bengali, 'is *shyambarna* and not *ujjwal shyambarna*'. Crudely translated, it meant that her daughter had the typical Indian complexion and she wouldn't couch it in any euphemism by describing her in any other way. My mother-in-law was different and stood out in our eyes.

This was unheard of in those days and even today where we, as a race, are enamoured, or to put it differently, fixated, by the fair skin. Pick up any matrimonial pull-out in any of today's leading dailies (irrespective of the state) and browse through the 'brides wanted section' and you would come across a majority of classifieds that go something like this:

'Wanted fair, thin, and well-cultured girl for Brahmin boy, 26, 5'8", working with MNC, currently in Bangalore, six-figure income and own flat. Interested parties may...'

My mother's mind was made up that instance. She told Baba that she would like none other than this particular girl as the bride for her younger son. Baba wasn't so sure. All marriage negotiations don't always go the way we want, but he stuck to his principle that they would entertain no further queries till we had exhausted this.

Baba hated the practice of juggling with multiple profiles of would-be 'brides', comparing and contrasting each against the other. If asked, he would reply irritatingly, 'I am not in the market trading cattle that I need to look up a whole herd while comparing teeth and hooves,' leaving the enquirer somewhat embarrassed.

One rarely messed with Baba when it came to questions on propriety, probity and values.

These values left an indelible imprint on my mind and I have later in my life attempted to hold on to them as steadfastly as possible. Baba taught me early on to never let go of one's value systems as he often said, 'You might lose it all some day, but it shall all come back to you. Should you lose your value systems, be sure that something which will never come back to you…it is like losing your very soul to the devil.'

Sixteen

RANJANA STEPPED INTO MY LIFE in the cold winter of Delhi on 10 March 1978.

Strange as it may sound, I met Ranjana for the second time during our elaborate wedding ceremony, which lasted for three–four days with rituals taking place at both our houses. Unlike today, Bengalis didn't, in general, have an engagement ceremony, the oral agreement between the families being enough to seal the bond. Families were honour-bound to stick by their word and most did unless their wards sprang a surprise lover at the last minute—something that was not unheard of.

Thus, the bride and the groom first laid their eyes on each other at the wedding venue and that too, during one of the many rituals. We had no mobile phones, landline phones itself being rare, let alone Facebook or WhatsApp to get to know our prospective partners.

Back in those days, young persons betrothed to each other were not encouraged to meet before the wedding took place; only to be broken by the undying romantics by exchanging furtive letters (addressed to their friend's house) or by telephone by the lucky ones.

We relied on the two persons on this earth who knew the best and worst in us and always carried our interests at heart.

It was an exciting and surreal time in my life. I suddenly had to share my space with someone whom I hardly knew. I often pitied my young bride for being suddenly uprooted from her familiar surroundings and thrown into the other end of the country to make a new life with an unknown man. I tried to make her as comfortable as I could. My sharing of space then seemed minuscule for the trouble that Ranjana took to make a home and hearth for me and build a life anew for herself after having lost her mother—someone she was extremely devoted to.

As the days rolled by, we got to know and like each other. At times, we were as different as chalk and cheese. We were bound by a deep respect for each other's differences as we were drawn closer by things that we shared in common. We came from entirely different family backgrounds. She was unafraid to speak her mind and lunged into debates with old and young alike for what she believed to be true. I, in sharp contrast, would always fall silent in diffidence to the elders and never could push my point across.

She got along famously with my mother and later on with my father who treated her as the daughter that he never had. We were a creatively bent couple and I fell in love with her voice. Schooled in the traditional Indian classical music system from Gandharva Mahavidyalaya—still among the best schools to learn Indian classical music—she excelled in singing songs of the poet Kavi Nazrul Islam, the national poet of Bangladesh.

Nazrul's writings explored themes such as love, freedom, humanity, divinity and revolution. More significantly, he was the pioneer of a new music system that took shape in the form of Bengali ghazals—an adaptation of the hugely popular Persian/Urdu poetic form. Ghazals are essentially poetic expressions, in the form of rhyming couplets and a refrain, each line sharing the same meter, and deal with the pain of separation. Originating in Arabia long before the advent of Islam, it was made popular in South Asia by travelling Sufi mystics.

A large number of Nazrul's ghazals were set to various ragas from the Indian classical music system and blended well with Ranjana's musical schooling. My hours at the club dwindled significantly as I spent many evenings in the company of my new bride and Ma, enveloped in her music.

All my apprehensions, however ridiculous they seem now as I reflect back, were washed away by her quiet, yet forceful demeanour and the sound of her music filling the room.

I saw yet another facet of Ma as she accompanied me along with my young bride to Vizag. She had come along to help Ranjana set up house and give her much-needed companionship during the long hours that I was away at work.

Ma chose to take on all the household chores on herself, shooing me and Ranjana away during the evenings saying, 'What are you young people doing at home in the evening? Go on and enjoy yourself.'

We went out on long rides on my bike or at times yielded to the temptation of spending the evening at the beach, looking at the sun going down over the endless expanse of water of the Bay of Bengal, the fading orb kissing a golden goodbye to the waves as they rushed to our feet.

Our sojourns would invariable end with a quick snack at a restaurant. At times we had no money to order two dosas and yet found indescribable joy in splitting a dosa between us. It felt good to be young and alive.

As I reflect back, I realise that those were the most enjoyable and fun-filled days of my life. Sure, we were stretched for money and I spent more than I had, but life threw no curve balls at us. Life was pure and had no complexities. There was nothing that one had to worry about. We were happy even when we had nothing.

ᴄᴧᴐ

Seventeen

In RANJANA, I FOUND A companionship that I had longed for. As the world went to sleep, we spent countless hours in the dark talking about ourselves and reconciling the different worlds that we came from. I had by then shifted houses and we had a room to ourselves and could afford to give Ma her independent bedroom and space.

As we lay enveloped in the darkness, interrupted at times by the incessant chirping of crickets, I opened myself up to my new friend. I spoke about Baba and Ma, my days at IIT and my love for all things creative. We discovered each other's pet peeves and likings. We spoke in hushed tones about Ma's fastidiousness and her broader views on life.

Ranjana found it intriguing that I had almost no one that I could call as a friend from my school days—someone with whom I would have shared the most intimate of confidences and secrets—as she reeled off the names of her friends, right from her kindergarten days up until her college days. That night, I gave her a glimpse into Baba's life and how it affected his own life as it affected his children's.

Baba had, in some ways, an unhappy childhood. The unhappiness manifested by Baba gave me a rich insight into the working of a child's mind and how words and expressions leave deep and lasting impressions—impressions and insecurities that one carries forward in their life. I needed no introduction to Freudian literature to understand the world that Baba had created for himself.

The youngest of three siblings, Baba had lost his mother when he was all of five years. Baba's dad, who was by then a well-established doctor, took the hit the hardest. He couldn't reconcile to the tragic loss of his wife and turned into a virtual recluse, disappearing for weeks and months on end at the hospital, shunning his household and family.

Too young to fathom the changing world around him, Baba was seen as the loose end of the equation and a decision was soon taken, within the extended family, to send him along to his maternal grandmother's house to be brought up.

Uprooted from his familiar surroundings and siblings, away from the comfort of his family, Baba suddenly found himself as the newest member of an alien family surrounded by five cousins. He must have also missed being in the midst of his own siblings.

His grandmother and aunt took it upon themselves to rear the child as their own and did their best to play the role of the mother that Baba so evidently missed and he, in turn, never forgot to mention them. To be fair, Baba's maternal uncle also treated him extremely well, denying him none of the material comforts that the two extended to their own children, but Baba was, in his child's mind, an outsider; someone who was thrust upon the family.

Having lost his mother at an impressionable age, Baba hung onto each and every word that was spoken in the household and filed them away to be brooded on later.

Baba used to speak at length about his childhood, which was at most times tinged with shades of indignation, self-pity and a deep sense of loss. As he grew up, he had convinced himself to the thought that he belonged to no one and nothing belonged to him.

I realised, as I grew older, that we often tend to relegate the 'good' that happens to us in the farther reaches of our memory, choosing to retain in vivid detail snippets of stray incidents and episodic conversations that had left us feeling hurt and betrayed. We could all do away with a lot of hurt and angst if we were to pause for a moment and reflect on the 'good' that rules our lives.

Baba carried forward his childhood impressions well into his adulthood, which then manifested itself in a multiplicity of ways—some good and some downright negative.

The lingering sense of life's injustices meant that Baba got swayed by Marx and identified personally with deep Leftist ideals. It bode well with his extremely emotional bent of mind. He resented inequality in any form. He saw things as starkly black and white or as good and bad.

He left no room for life's varied shades of grey.

As he entered manhood, he did not shy away from calling a spade a spade and built around him a world that was ruled by propriety, the rule of law and a deep yearning for an egalitarian world; he eschewed any signs of wealth and appeared stung by it. This aversion to money and wealth perhaps sprung from being uprooted at a tender age and put in the midst of a wealthy foster family that gave him all material comforts but failed to assuage his feeling of rootlessness and the need for belonging.

Again, his conviction that he belonged to no one and nothing belonged to him manifested itself in a wholly different way when Dadamoni, my elder brother and his first child, was born. He clung to Dadamoni with a strange ferocity and would virtually let no one come between them—not even his wife, the child's mother. It was as if he had finally found 'something' or 'someone' that was truly his—someone who was a part of his flesh and blood and belonged to him and none other.

He let go of that ferocious sense of belonging when I was born, but then my young mind took to understanding things differently. To me it seemed, childish as it sounds now, that Baba paid more attention to Dadamoni and cared more dearly for him—attentive to his every need—not that I was neglected in any way, leaving me to my own devices.

As we talked that night, Ranjana in her characteristic uninhibited way gave me a wholly different perspective to the whole thing. Propping herself on her elbow, she looked at me and said, 'You have a misplaced sense of sadness. Didn't it strike you that Baba's clinging to Dadamoni was beyond the normal? With you, he did what an average parent would do...let you discover yourself without binding you in chains!'

Baba's sense of propriety and honesty often got him into scraps with people, both at work and outside. At times, we were embarrassed by his indignant outbursts and found it hard to hold him back.

Baba's fastidiousness for probity and honesty in public life caused him to get headlong into arguments with his superiors, which was not taken lightly. They had their vengeance by transferring him around the country, which meant we had to pack up our bags at short notices and lug ourselves to a new city every few years.

This also meant that I studied in no less than nine different schools during my 12 years of formal schooling, which resulted in me having neither friends nor fond memories of school life. I had no one I could confide in and carried a feeling of rootlessness. In some ways, I became a reflection of Baba when it came to emotions—something that I am not very adept at handling.

Baba's difficult childhood and emotional vulnerability found expression in his creative and literary pursuits. He felt most at peace with himself and his world seemed settled then. It also resulted in his deep love for children and later on in life, for divinity.

By the time he had entered his 40s, he grew tired of raging a lone battle with a world that he viewed as one steeped in the pursuit of wealth by all means, fair and foul, and increasingly locked himself in his literary pursuits. This was the most productive phase of his life where he penned a large anthology of poems with children as his primary audience. He would later go on to compose a large compendium of devotional songs after the loss of his wife—a blow that he would, like his father, find extremely difficult to come to terms with.

Among his most notable work for children were *Biliti Chhara*, where he translated popular English rhymes into Bengali, giving Bengali children a rare insight into the rich world of English rhymes that resonated well with the audience of the time.

His other notable and widely popular collections for children included *Saradiya Chhara* (Poems on the Festive Season), *Ghum Bhanganir Chhara* (Early Morning Poems) and *Chhara Diilam Chhoriye* (A Spread of Poems).

◆

As kids, Dadamoni and I would find it difficult to appreciate Baba's fastidiousness for probity and honesty, sometimes wondering why he created such a hue and cry about things. Two distinctly different instances come to mind.

The first incident that comes vividly to mind took place in Delhi and I must have been all of 10 or 11 years of age.

We had boarded a bus to take us from our government quarters in R.K. Puram to Connaught Place for an evening outing when, out of the blue, Baba got into a mighty scrape with the conductor. All flushed and red in the face, he was shouting, 'You cannot talk to a lady like this... you should know better and talk to a lady with respect...' and he railed on. The conductor appeared to be taken aback by this angry outburst, unable to fathom what caused it. It dawned on us that the fellow had egged on a female passenger to disembark faster in his characteristic and somewhat rustic Haryanvi accent, which seemed to Baba both insolent and disrespectful. The poor fellow was only speaking the tongue that he knew and meant no harm.

We were left feeling embarrassed as the rest of the passengers stared at us, with Ma trying her best to pacify her man.

The other incident took place in Lucknow, in the midst of the hot and sweltering summer season. This was also the time for mangoes—a fruit that Dadamoni and I particularly relished.

One day, as we sat hanging around the veranda with nothing to occupy us, a man from Baba's office came through the gates bearing a large basket laden with ripe mangoes. The subordinate had travelled to his native village and had brought back with him a generous stash of mangoes to be distributed to the city folk.

Baba had spied the fellow from afar and came rushing out of the house. 'What is this?' he thundered, pointing at the mangoes.

'Some mangoes from my village for the little babu sahibs,' the fellow muttered as he sheepishly pointed to the basket full of ripe mangoes.

'*Tumhara gaon kab se Hazratgunj hone laga?* (When did Hazratgunj become your village?)' my father bellowed at the poor fellow. '*Aam bazaar se laate ho aur bolte ho gaon ka aam hai* (You buy mangoes from the bazaar and claim that it's from your village),' he hollered, finally shooing away the petrified fellow with the firm injunction never to come bearing gifts of fruit, or for that matter anything else, to a senior's residence.

Dadamoni and I looked on in dismay as the man bearing the basket of ripe mangoes disappeared rapidly from view. We thoroughly rued the loss of a treat, but then who was to reason with Baba!

∽

Eighteen

ON FRIDAY, 13 APRIL 1979, Ranjana gifted me with a lovely set of twin sons. As I cradled the tiny bundled-up humans in my arms, I let out a silent prayer thanking Him for his bounty and keeping the children and mother safe. At precisely that moment, the twins let out a mighty wail as if to signify their presence on earth. We had firmly entered the hallowed portals of parenthood.

The thought of being a father had come with a great deal of trepidation and a good measure of excitement. How does one prepare for parenthood, I wondered. Where does one ferret the right information from? These and a hundred other questions buzzed around my head as I went about life waiting for D-Day.

I sorely needed someone by Ranjana's side and we canvassed relatives on both sides since my mother, who had not been keeping well lately, was ruled out from undertaking such a lengthy journey and also taking on the strain of caring for the newborn babies and their mother.

Ranjana's elder sister, whom we all called Didibhai, readily agreed to come and stay with us. I heaved a sigh of relief. A matronly lady, she took over the duties of caring for Ranjana from the moment that she stepped in and stayed with us for over six months after Rahul and Romit, as we were to christen the twins, were born. She selflessly gave up her own family life and comfort for our sake—an act for which we couldn't thank her enough till this day. But for her support, we would have been lost.

I grew more and more anxious as the D-Day drew closer, as perhaps all first-time dads are, and fretted about Ranjana till I made such a nuisance of myself that Didibhai had to finally shoo me away saying, 'Why don't you go to the club and spend time with your friends?' I thanked Didibhai for that and made myself scarce, but was soon back home, unable to tear myself away for long hours. Agitated as I was, I gave myself frightful moments imagining the darkest possibilities. What if I misjudged the timing and was late in rushing Ranjana to the hospital? What if the child decided to come out early? What if the water broke while I was away at work? What if the vehicle broke down midway? My fertile mind imagined possibilities galore.

I finally decided that I had had enough of the dark clouds swirling over my head and got Ranjana admitted to King George Hospital, the best one then in Vizag, some good five days before the ordained day. Costs be damned, I told myself as I booked her into a single room, Didibhai in tow. 'Between you and the doctors, she is now in safe hands,' I told Didibhai, grinning, happy that my dark broodings were now amply assuaged.

Soon enough, the appointed day arrived and I parked myself in the hospital from the wee hours of the morning. Ranjana, cheerful as ever, signalled all was well as she was wheeled into the delivery room on a gurney, leaving me to pace about the corridor in nervous excitement.

In time, a couple of other expectant mothers were also wheeled into the delivery room and we had quite a motley group of would-be dads pacing about the long corridor, some of us disappearing for a smoke but quickly returning, having only half a cigarette and squishing the still half-burning cigarette with our shoes in our nervous excitement and eagerness not to be found missing for lengthy stretches.

It was not long before I could hear sounds of steady moaning coming from the delivery room. The moaner seemed in a great deal of pain and let out heart-wrenching groans every now and then. In a while, I couldn't bear the sounds any longer and moved myself to the other end of the corridor, keeping a keen eye on the closed door.

As I looked up my watch, I realised that it was nearing four hours since Ranjana had been wheeled in and I still saw no signs of her or the baby. There were a couple of nurses scurrying about, entering and leaving the room, but none of the doctors were in sight.

In a while, a nurse came out cradling a wailing infant and my heart missed a beat as she announced the name of the father. A wave of disappointment washed over me as I realised it was not my name that was being called out but another Bengali gentleman's.

It had been six hours since the first contractions had begun and there was still no sign of Ranjana. The steady sound of moaning could still be heard emanating from the delivery room. I couldn't hold myself back any longer and waylaid a nurse on one of her many trips to the room. I asked for Ranjana and was hurriedly told that she was still under active labour. 'You can hear her moaning,' she added, trying to be helpful.

It felt as if I had been punched in the stomach. Too stunned to react, I slumped into the nearest chair. All the while, I had been thinking that it was some other lady who was letting out those heart-wrenching groans. I felt sick and mildly nauseous. The whole atmosphere suddenly started feeling claustrophobic, leaving me gasping for air.

I rushed out and drove straight to the beach. I couldn't think of anywhere else to go. As I watched the sun going down over the horizon, I looked up at the crimson red sky and let out a fervent prayer to God. 'O Lord,' I prayed, 'why are you taking the poor girl through such suffering. She has done no harm. Please let me be the one to suffer.'

I picked myself from the beach after an hour and drove back to the hospital, resuming my long watch. It was a little past 3 p.m. that Ranjana gave birth to the twins. The eldest, Rahul, was born five minutes before his twin Romit let out an almighty wail on entering the world.

ॐ

Nineteen

THE TWINS WERE NEARLY 11 months old when I got my first promotion at Indian Oxygen and was transferred to Hyderabad. This meant moving my young family, lock, stock and barrel, to a new city of which I knew nothing.

I dreaded the thought of house hunting in a new city while I left the twins—who were quite a handful now—to be chaperoned by their mother. As I mulled over possible solutions to get me out of this fix, it struck me that Abhindra, my school and IIT KGP mate with whom I was in intermittent touch, was at that time with the Defence Research and Development Organisation (DRDO) and, as luck would have, posted in Hyderabad.

Ranjana and I decided that it would be best to seek his advice and maybe he could point us to a suitable house that might just be ready to move into.

It would not have been more than four or five days before I heard back from Abhindra. I marvelled at the efficiency of the post office, since letters were known to go missing for weeks, if not months.

True to Abhindra's style and large-heartedness, he would settle for nothing less than hosting us at his place, and to quote him, '...we must not rush into the task of looking for a house. House hunting is serious business and we must take our own time over it...'

Thus, we moved to Hyderabad and into Abhindra's abode. By then, he was married to his lady love Sushmita, whom we called Shuma for short, and had been blessed with a son.

The eight of us—Abhindra's mother was also staying with him—crammed into his modest quarters, but none of us minded the lack of space. We were, as if, thrown back to our IIT KGP days, albeit with families of our own.

Abhindra's large-heartedness was legendary among his IIT KGP mates. He used to be the guy who ran up the largest bills with Sadhu, never thinking twice about throwing an impromptu treat of mango lassi during the hot summers. A tall fellow, he would tower over the rest and with an extended arm hand over the tall glasses to be relayed to the thirsty crowd, all the while telling Sadhu, 'Ekta aaro dao (hand me one more).'

He was excited at the prospect of hosting us and it came not from a sense of friendship or duty but a strange sort of altruism, following the age-old Sanskrit dictum of 'Athithi devo bhava (the guest is equivalent to God)'. The factually precise meaning of the dictum wholly applied to Abhindra which states, 'be the one for whom the guest is God'—a guest that has no fixed date of arrival nor departure.

Abhindra's excitement, almost child-like in its enthusiasm, was highly contagious. It became a routine for us to scour the local markets hunting for the freshest veggies and, of course, the freshest catch of the day. He wouldn't let me reach for my wallet, let alone shell out cash, stonewalling my attempts by gripping my wrist, saying, 'All in good time, Biku (that being my nickname)… you too shall have your opportunity to host me… for now I am your elder and the host.'

We ended up spending some two months with Abhindra before we were reluctantly allowed to move to a rented house some 15 minutes away from his perch.

Dinner times were the most memorable during our long stay with him. Abhindra was fastidious when it came to the one major meal of the day and insisted all of us eat together, the children having been put to bed by then.

Shuma was the perfect hostess and we would sit for hours reminiscing about our days at Durgapur and IIT KGP. Shuma too was from Durgapur and a few years younger to Abhindra. We never tired regaling our friends with their love story and early courtship days.

It was Abhindra who had first spied upon Shuma as she went about shopping with her gaggle of girlfriends in a market that we used to often frequent. Abhindra fell for the sweet lady there and then, but lacked the courage to walk up to her and introduce himself.

The next evening, the gang assembled at Bapi da's place, our regular *adda* haunt, with a purpose. Abhindra's lady love needed to be traced, her name discovered, her antecedents dug up and her routine revealed. We acted as proper detectives and divided ourselves into teams that fanned out across town. We soon discovered Abhindra's love to be Sushmita Mukherjee, who hailed from a good middle-class Brahmin family and happened to be an excellent dancer.

We had by now gained a fair degree of insight into Shuma's movements and planned a fortuitous meeting at one of the block markets. True to routine, we happened to cross paths with her as she made her evening appearance at the market. It had befallen upon me to execute the next step in our mission and thus without any further ado, I walked up to her and introduced myself and Abhindra, whom I had dragged alone. Her smile gave her away and from then on we went on to become fast friends, weathering some of the most tumultuous events in our lives.

Life passed by at an easy pace in Hyderabad and I yearned for some serious action. It didn't quite suit my temperament to cruise along in autopilot mode and wait for my next promotion. My first promotion had come by fairly quickly, perhaps aided in large measure by the report that I had written on the Bailadila mining project that had been addressed directly to the desk of the managing director of Indian Oxygen. In fact, the managing director, Mr S.D. Singh, an extremely smart Punjabi gentleman, had made it a point to single out Ranjana, only a few months into our marriage, during an official party thrown in his honour on his visit to Vizag, and patting me on the shoulder, had said, 'You have married a fine man, madam...I see in him the makings of a CEO of Indian Oxygen one day.'

One day, while I was deeply engrossed in the morning newspaper, the twins waddling about me, blabbering to themselves in their make-believe play world, I chanced upon an impressive recruitment advert from Hindustan Computers Ltd (HCL) looking for bright and energetic sales managers for its rapidly expanding computer business.

I knew nothing about computers then, which was a technological novelty at that time, as were aeroplanes during our parents' days. But something about the design of the advert and the language it was drafted in greatly appealed to me and I applied for the position without a second thought.

It came naturally to me, given my proclivity to deep dive into the unknown, largely unmindful of the risks that it involved. I didn't think twice about leaving the sheltered bay of Indian Oxygen. Not even the twins or my young family came to mind. Where men would have seen turbulence and shied away from the rough and tumble of an untested upstart private industry, I saw only opportunity and growth.

I started to realise that's me.

Once an IITian, always an IITian.
Bikram after his graduation, at IIT Kharagpur

Left-handed magic.
Paddler Bikram in full flow at IIT Kharagpur

Bikram (fourth from left) along with Indian Oxygen's Managing Director S.D. Singh (third from left) and other company officials at Waltair Club, Vizag (1978)

Bikram (fourth from left) and his colleagues from Indian Oxygen, Vizag, pose with the inter-zonal cup for best performance (1978). Also seen are Bikram's first boss, V. Balagopalan (second from left) and Regional Manager (South) A.K. Bhattacharya (first from right)

*Bikram in the hot seat of the office
Willys Jeep in Vizag (1977)*

*Bikram (right) along with
(from left) his elder brother Dr
Arjun Dasgupta (Dadamoni),
father Sukamal Dasgupta,
sister-in-law Kajal (Boudi)
and mother Kalyani (1974)*

Bikram (fourth from left) and members of the
Bengali Association Club in Vizag celebrate the Bengali New Year (1978)

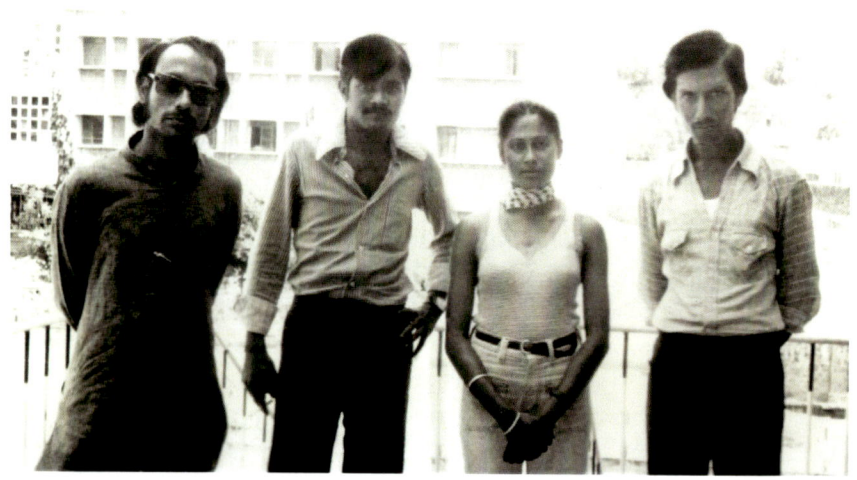

Bengali Association Club's Film Society hosts celebrated actor Smita Patil in Vizag (1975)
Smita is flanked on the left by Bikram and Ratan Kumar Pal, general secretary,
Bengali Association Club on the right

All India Contract Bridge Tournament at the Ordinance Factory Board (OFB).
A PCL team, led by Bikram, designed the computer software for the tournament

Client server architecture on display, for the first time in India
at CSI '90, by the PCL team led by Bikram (1990)

The then Prime Minister P.V. Narasimha Rao along with Bikram walk through the PCL pavilion at IT Asia '93 in New Delhi (1993)

Bikram speaks at the inaugural session of IT Asia '94 in New Delhi (1994)

Bikram (fourth from left) at IT Asia '93 in New Delhi (1993) is flanked by (from left) MAIT's (Manufacturers' Association for Information Technology) Secretary General, Vijay Chopra; MAIT's President, Ashok Soota; MAIT's Vice-President, K.R. Palta; Ashok Advani, owner of Business India Publications; and Nalin Kohli

A typical BAIT (Beer Drinkers' Association of Information Technology) retreat (1995). Bikram (second from left) with Nandan Nilekani, Vijaya Raghavan, Anil Batra, Pravin Gandhi, Vijay Singh Thakur, Dinesh Puri and others

The BAIT Founders. Bikram with (from left to right)
Vijay Raghavan, Pradeep Kar and Pravin Gandhi (2010)

The Family
From left: Oindrila (Romit's wife), Mishka (Romit's daughter), Romit (Bikram's son),
Ranjana (Bikram's wife), Rahul (Bikram's son) and Janine (Rahul's wife)

Limelight

One

I GOT OFF FROM THE AUTO-RICKSHAW and stood for a moment on the wide red-stoned pavement, blowing into my cupped hands, trying to get life back into my fingers numbed by the cold Delhi air. I sorely needed a cigarette but perished the thought, not wanting to reek of tobacco, not during my maiden interview with HCL.

I asked my way around the maze of towers that made up Nehru Place, not yet the buzzing business district that it has come to be, and found myself at the ground floor of Siddharth Building as the lift creaked and squawked on its way down.

It took me two attempts before I could finally find a place for myself in the lift as it moaned its way up, grudging every stop on the way. It took almost an eternity to reach the eighth floor, which gave me enough time to rehearse my opening spiel when I abruptly recalled what Mr Balagopalan had advised me when I had taken him into confidence about my decision to appear for the HCL interview.

'Well, Bikram,' he had started, with his characteristic wink, 'IOL is a known devil and HCL an unknown angel. Your life and career depends on who you would like to bank upon—the known devil or an unknown angel.' And that was all that he ever spoke on the subject as he signed off on my leave requisition.

I chose to follow in the tread of the unknown angel.

As I entered the small meeting room, I was greeted by a tall, well-built gentleman. I froze for a moment as we both looked at each other in mutual recognition. 'You TT!' exclaimed the genial giant, deftly flicking away an imaginary table tennis ball into the air with his hand, as he rose from behind the table.

The gentleman was Arjun Malhotra, three batches my senior at IIT

KGP, and one of the six founders of HCL.

It didn't seem to be like any job interview that I had ever attended, with Arjun taking on the mantle of an affectionate elder brother, as we swapped our life stories. I listened on in fascination as Arjun took me through the last few years of his entrepreneurial journey.

'Entrepreneurship is fun, Bikram,' said Arjun as he directed the peon to fetch us some tea. 'It is exciting to be able to read the air and foretell with a degree of conviction and mulishness of purpose what the future holds, and it is here that we might have scored over the monolith DCM,' he added, giving me a huge grin. Arjun hated pontificating.

It was at Delhi Cloth Mills (DCM) that the six young men had floated the concept of a 'computer', a device that was much more than an intelligent calculator, as the next big breakthrough in the market and had gone on to develop the first of the rudimentary 8-bit and 16-bit microprocessors to power their machines.

'It helped HCL's cause immensely that we were named Hindustan Computers Ltd, which unwitting customers took as a government-run concern and as a replacement to the might of IBM. We neither denied nor affirmed the assumption, our boys haw-humming whenever the subject cropped up,' grinned Arjun, as he gingerly sipped the piping hot tea.

'And as luck would have it, our full-page newspaper advertisement launching our maiden computing product in August 1977 was sweetly juxtaposed between banner headlines announcing the withdrawal of International Business Machines (IBM) from June 1978,' he said, beaming ear to ear.

This first of its kind, a 'Make in India' product, derived solely from native research and development, was in sharp contrast to the prevalent practice of assembling or importing fully built-up machines to be sold in the domestic market. This in many ways was a precursor to building a strong backbone for the IT sector in India.

HCL's 8C stood out in the market for a variety of reasons and came out at the same time as its counterparts in US—a stunning feat for a home-grown start-up. It sported, for the first time, a 5.28-inch floppy drive system with a storage capacity of 80 kilobytes (KB) where the 8-inch floppy discs were the rage with machine manufacturers. Married with it was the Power Shut Auto Restart (PSAR) Unit, capable of running on a car battery, and which came along with a matching software utility that ensured protection from power outages by restarting the program from where it was interrupted.

'You see, Bikram,' Arjun continued, as he drew me back to the present, 'now that IBM has started re-exploring the Indian computing market again, we have upped our game.'

Arjun went on to describe how the first 'computer', as we now know it, had been developed and was due to be launched nationwide. 'This time around, we have decided to adopt Microsoft's DOS, the Disc Operating System, as the operating system instead of the CP/M, Control Program/Monitor, operating system that we have been using so far. My bet would be that we will see DOS to be around for some time and since it has some features that it shares with CP/M, WordStar and dBase would likely be easily ported to it.'

It all sounded bewildering to me. I still hadn't come across a computer, let alone know what Arjun meant when he had reeled off those terms. As Arjun came to a halt, I voiced my concern.

'But, I know nothing about computers, Molly...' (I was used to referring to Arjun by his pet name from his IIT days).

'Neither do I!' he responded with a warm smile. I must have looked somewhat bemused as he came over and rested his hands on my shoulders to reassure me saying, 'Come on in, Bikram.'

To Arjun, it hardly mattered that I was unschooled in 'computers'—that was something which could be easily overcome. What mattered was the common brotherhood that we shared—that meant familiarity, stability and a certain degree of trust.

Shiv Nadar, the undisputed leader among the six founders, stood out in sharp contrast. A master strategist, he was gifted with the knack of taking an extremely detached view of things. For Shiv, winning was everything as he went about his task with a degree of ruthlessness and extreme focus that is rare to come across. He cut no corners, neither did he give any.

Two

I JOINED THE START-UP HCL in early 1981 as IBM started sniffing around the Indian market to sell its own brand of computers. They would formally enter Indian shores in February 1992 in collaboration with the Tatas as Tata Information Systems Ltd.

Stepping into HCL then meant entering a whole new world. A world that bubbled over with youthful energy and a searing fire to make something out of yourself while dallying with cutting-edge technologies of the day.

During those early days of fervent excitement, none of us felt like an employee. We were entrepreneurs within an entrepreneurial ecosystem, raring to rule the world, mentored by the likes of Shiv Nadar, Arjun Malhotra, and Amit Dutta Gupta.

The first few months at HCL, Delhi, went by in a blur. My life revolved around understanding the fundamentals of computing. System 2, the newest 8-bit computer whose launch was on the anvil, had us all excited. The newness of the technology meant that we had to improvise how we positioned and sold our products. With both buyers and sellers equally in the dark, it gave rise to hilarious sales situations and called for some sharp thinking. With my brief training period at Delhi drawing to a close, I was posted to Calcutta as the business development manager. It is here that I met my mentor and guide in Dadan Bhai, who was to shape my life from then on. As the regional manager (East), he had recently moved into HCL's posh new office at 45, Jhautala Road. Not too far away from the business district, the four-storeyed building housed HCL's software division on the first floor, while the second floor was taken up by the marketing and sales offices.

Dadan Bhai had been deputed to Calcutta to head the eastern flank after an eventful stint in Guwahati, heading the Northeast operations for

HCL with aplomb.

Born into a well-to-do family from the hinterlands of Bihar, Dadan Bhai was perhaps the only one from his village to enter an IIT in the 1960s. He had taken up agricultural engineering, dreaming of transforming farming practices back in his village.

But age-old practices die hard and his elder brother, entrenched in a heavily patriarchal and ritualistic society, prevailed upon him and his new ideas. It must have been with a heavy heart that he found himself back in the din and bustle of a city again, as a banker with the Bank of India.

I haven't met a more aggressive and enterprising mentor, salesman, entrepreneur and creative hustler than Dadan Bhai. There will be no second Dadan Bhai. His is a mantle difficult to wear. For all his rustic background, he had one of the sharpest minds on the block and could put to shame many a sleek city folk with their gilded English accents. He carried no pretences and bore grudges like the knights of yore.

We hit it off like a pair of Siamese twins as soon as we met. I was taken in by his rustic charm and unfettered aggression, and he perhaps thought well of my ability to speak English well and swing it with the clients.

Buoyed by his exploits in the Northeast, it was perhaps only Dadan Bhai who could fill the void left on the eastern front by another stalwart, Amit Dutta Gupta, who had by 1981 moved to New Delhi to head the marketing team with Arjun Malhotra pulling up the national sales flank.

I moved along with my family to Kolkata (earlier Calcutta) in mid-1981 and got down to what would be the start to the most happening phase of my work life.

If life in Vizag had followed a familiar pattern, HCL turned out to be its mirror opposite. My days were consumed in traversing through the entire eastern region scouting for customers, particularly vying to bag large institutional orders from a slew of public sector organisations that HCL had christened OSCAR (Oil, Steel, Coal and Railways).

Winning an order from an OSCAR account called for wild celebrations. It felt like being in a tribe infested with Spartan soldiers each vying for the fabled Olympic olive wreath.

It was during this period that HCL came out with possibly its most memorable marketing campaign; the brainchild of Amit Dutta Gupta, the series of five full-page nationwide advertisements went on to change the face of the computing market in India.

If we were to write paeans to celebrate the life and times of the early stalwarts of the IT industry in India, the richest of the verses would be perhaps reserved for the unsung hero of it all—Amit Dutta Gupta, whom I and a host of other young men called Amit da, both in awe and respect. His ideas and deep understanding of the consumer psyche did more to launch the IT industry than anyone else's.

If Bill Gates' Microsoft Disk Operating System (MS-DOS) brought home the power of the computer to the common user, it was Amit Dutta Gupta's keen foresight that foresaw the coming revolution in IT and veered HCL away from using UNIX-based proprietary operating systems to adopting MS-DOS, helping bring about the personal computer (PC) revolution in India.

If I had picked up the fine art of salesmanship from Dadan Bhai during his stint with HCL, it was at Amit da's feet that I learned all about marketing and understanding customer psyche. One couldn't have had a more erudite, quietly confident man than Amit da as one's mentor when one is in the most vulnerable stage of one's work life, and words often sound shallow when it comes to describing him.

Those young men who were under his tutelage went on to create history on their own, firmly clasping the first seeds of success bestowed on them by their guru—an outstanding testament to the genius of the giant among men.

Most organisations of some size back then had what was called the EDP or electronic data processing department to manage their internal IT needs and were manned by a handful of persons who knew what computers were and proved to be tough nuts to crack. So were the early adopters of the unit record machines (URM), the precursor to the modern electronic computer. URMs allowed for complex data processing tasks such as accounting. These tasks were accomplished by processing punch cards in a particular sequence through the URMs.

Most of the user segment, as we know today, viewed computers as esoteric machines that were highly complicated and called for specialist operators. This mindset dissuaded large tracts of potential buyers from investing in computers, which was further compounded by the high prices of the machines. It was some 18 times cheaper to buy an Ambassador car than lug home a computer!

To Amit da, it presented a fascinating challenge. Along with Shiv, Arjun and Raman, who commandeered the technology and production flank, worked on the idea of opening up the primary market consisting of first-time users, while ensuring that they could access the machines without burning a hole in their pockets. Thus, it was as much a game of prising open an entirely new and highly challenging market segment as it was of assiduous pricing.

So, as the team trudged on, Amit da intuitively moved away from the staid technical jargon-laced advertisements of the day and came up with the brilliant 'Exploding the common computer myth: Too complicated my staff cannot handle it' campaign with the signature line: 'Even your typist can operate'—a line that became synonymous with computer marketing and practically every other kind of product positioning.

Shiv, on the other hand, arrived buoyant from his meeting with the Industrial Development Bank of India (IDBI), armed with a soft financing scheme that enabled potential buyers to invest in computers on easy purchase terms. They hit the market under the same banner series of 'Exploding the common computer myth: It costs too much money' campaign with a full-page advertisement screaming 'Now you can buy a computer for as little as ₹3,500 a month', for a machine that cost upwards of ₹4.5 lakh.

The campaign burst upon the market as a huge bombshell, sending the competition scurrying into their bunkers and prising open Amit da's much cherished primary market. For the first time in the history of the Indian computer market, first-time users stirred from their slumber and saw the potential in investing in computers.

In a single masterstroke, Amit da had moved the market away from the prissiness of EDP managers and URM devotees to the small and medium enterprise (SME) segment who at times invested in computers to keep up with competition and thus catapulted HCL to the top of the pile of IT companies in India.

☙

Three

Mornings started early at HCL. We would be ready at our outpost in 45, Jhautala Road by 8 a.m. or at times earlier for our daily sales briefing call with Arjun, who would invariably be by his phone at his Golf Links residence in New Delhi; incidentally, it was from the bedrooms of this residence that HCL started its garage operations.

With telephone lines as crackly as they were those days it was as if we were separated by oceans, our voices fading in and out, as we shouted back and forth into the black mouthpieces. We discussed a myriad sales issues and objections, the difficulty in convincing a particularly prickly customer or cribbed about production and delivery delays.

I have never seen Arjun lose his cool during such morning rituals. His calm voice would waft over the lines as he solved each and every issue right there and then. There was no waiting for tomorrow. It is to the credit of the man that he repeated this feat with each and every sales team from every region every morning.

I have always marvelled at this facility of Arjun's and his ability to keep his composure in the face of the severest of odds and challenges. No issue was too small or trivial to be discussed and making mistakes didn't call for lengthy pontificating, but an opportunity to redeem oneself in the next call.

Our days were consumed in pushing HCL's 'Even a typist can operate' a System 2 machine. With Dadan Bhai at the helm in the region, we scoured the market with a naked aggression that was the hallmark of HCL. Every day was a fresh battle that one went to—the scars of the last battle still seared in our memories. You fought to win and you didn't leave winning for another day. There was no place for being a No. 2 in our lives.

The desire not to succumb in the face of the heaviest of odds was what marked us as different from the others. Life was seen in stark binary terms—you either won or you lost.

It was HCL's aggression and nonchalant attitude towards competition that won us some of the most prized orders of the day. In one such instance IIT Bombay had, in the early 1980s, floated an RFP (request for proposals) for some 100-odd computers—to be awarded to the vendor who could match their technical requirements at the lowest price.

This was a large order by any standard and the competition, coming in all shapes and forms, vied for it and despatched power-packed delegations to Bombay for the ensuing negotiations. All the teams were naturally helmed by senior professionals of the rank of vice president and above. A supremely confident HCL sent in a one-man army in the form of a senior sales executive.

As the men gathered around the head of the purchase committee and its other distinguished members, piling them with all matter of technical and pricing information, our man, spying an opportune moment, strode up to the committee and in a quietly confident manner told a member, 'Please seek whatever information you deem fit from the rest of the competition and once you are done just let me know your desired specifications, which I will build into the contract along with your preferred price...' With that he walked back and sat through the entire discussion only to walk away with the order at the end of the day.

At HCL, sales persons were empowered enough to take decisions on the spot, while other companies were bogged down by layers of regimented command and control centres. This grassroots-level empowerment of its executives fostered a sense of supreme confidence in people who flowered in their later lives and helmed some of the most prominent organisations around the globe.

No wonder that HCL, over a period of time, has spawned hundreds of CEOs across the globe.

It was a great deal of fun selling new technology in an environment where the buyer and the seller were equally in the dark about the potential uses of the technology. If Amit da's sterling media campaign was gradually pushing us from a 'push' based sales environment to a 'pull' or demand-based market, there were also situations where thinking on your feet could result in higher sales outcomes.

I once accompanied Dadan Bhai to Guwahati, chasing a potential 11-computer deal from a fairly large government-run establishment. Dadan Bhai, in his usual rustic style, let me know his plan as we got off the train at Guwahati railway station.

'Dasgupta Seth,' he started (for some strange reason he always referred to me by this honorific title), as he directed the porter to lug our baggage, '*Aap toh aache angreji bol lete hai. Aap bolna aur close karne ki chinta mujh par chor dena* (Don't fret about closing the deal...you give your spiel in English, which you do very well, and leave the rest to me).' I smiled as I nodded in agreement.

We arrived handsomely prepared at the client office and were ushered into a large conference room. We were flanked on the other side by a jovial-looking purchase manager, a junior sidekick of his, the EDP manager and a senior systems executive.

Introductions over, the EDP manager and his executive gave us a run-down of their operations and were visibly proud of their bank of IBM-manufactured unit record machines. They were now on the hunt for data entry machines, using the latest technology of the day.

'These would be hard nuts to crack,' I thought as I launched into my sales pitch. I gave them a complete rundown of our System 2 and data entry machines, contrasting how much more powerful our microcomputer was in comparison to their existing hardware and waxed eloquent about higher productivity, zero data loss and so on.

The guys on the other end of the table nodded sagely, not wanting to appear lacking in their appreciation of the technology of the day which perhaps only HCL could sport.

Dadan Bhai, on the other hand, sat with his arms neatly folded on the table, looking at me and his audience in turns, at times nodding and smiling along with the EDP manager. He looked like a tiger ready to spring on its prey, but with an exterior that belied nothing.

By the time I had ended with my closing remarks, having answered whatever queries that they had, Dadan Bhai had spied his opening and without wasting a moment looked at the EDP manager and with a straight face said, 'But, sir, I wonder why are you ordering only 11 machines when you would really require to have 33 machines?'

There was dead silence in the room. It took a couple of seconds before the EDP manager came back with, 'But why, sir?'

'Don't you see, sir!' quipped Dadan Bhai, as if admonishing an errant child. 'With your kind of vast computing operation, you would need a bank of 11 data entry machines, and while the data entry progresses your staff can use the other bank of 11 machines to simultaneously carry on with data validation. You will double your productivity. The rest of the 11 machines will come in handy as standby machines should either of the data entry or validation machines fail and your guys left idle, setting your complex accounting and payroll work back by days,' he said, helpfully adding, 'it is electronics after all, one can never be too sure!'

The EDP manager had soaked in all that Dadan Bhai had said like a sponge. It dawned on him that he would really need 33 machines to cover his 11 operators, used to as he was with his URM logic of readers, verifiers and sorters. Little did the poor fellow realise at that instant that a single machine could be used both for data entry and verification and the standby machine was just what it was—a smokescreen.

He turned to look at his purchase manager who appeared puzzled by all this mumbo jumbo and said, 'Make out a purchase order for 33 machines' and returning his attention to us said, 'Sir, now that we are buying more machines, shouldn't we get some discount?'

I burst out into loud peals of laughter as we boarded the taxi back to the hotel. In one stroke, Dadan Bhai had increased his order basket three-fold as we merrily discussed how easy it was to get away with blue murder when it came to government-run organisations and their need to spend their budgetary allocations before it lapsed at the end of the fiscal year.

Private concerns fared no better and there were times when customers ordered machines that they had no need for. One of the best instances was narrated by Arjun.

An HCL executive had tapped into a fairly large bicycle manufacturer based in Ludhiana, Punjab, and had taken Arjun and Amit da along to understand the customer's key problem. After an intensive systems study, Amit da had derived that putting the firm's accounts payables in order would wipe out most of the severe ills plaguing the firm, helping streamline their production system. Armed with a thick dossier, they proposed an HCL 8/C Level 20 machine with two floppy drives.

The client pondered over the issue, marvelling at the promise of technology, and went on to query how many '*chakkas*' or floppy drives were there in the machine that HCL had sold to their competitors, Vardhman, which turned out to be an HCL 8/C Level 30 system sporting three-floppy drive system or three '*chakkas*' in the customer's parlance.

The client promptly ordered for a four '*chakka*' system—the HCL 8/C Level 44 machine with four floppy drives. So much so to keep ahead of the competition!

In another instance, a customer happened to ask Rajendra Pawar, or Raji as we called him, if they would need a two-floppy drive machine or a three-floppy drive machine. He gave it a great deal of thought, scratched his beard and looked up at the ceiling; finally, looking sagely at the customer, he said, 'Two will do, but three would be better for you!'

The customer never questioned what 'better' meant and he walked away happily armed with this new knowledge and a new computer to show.

✍

Four

BEHIND ALL THE EXCITEMENT AT HCL, the regimented pounding of the streets and seeing the eastern region rise to the top, there was a nagging worry that didn't let me be at peace with myself.

The twins were growing up at an alarming rate or so I thought since I was inclined to see a momentous change in them each time I returned to the city from a hectic tour of the provinces or the neighbouring states.

Of the two boys, Rahul was the weaker one and every time I saw him pottering around his brother, I found myself being thrown back to that fateful morning in Vizag.

It was early one morning when Rahul, who must have been some three to four months old, woke up wailing and sniffing, showing all symptoms of having caught a common cold. With Ranjana busy managing the household and his twin brother, I bundled up the little one in my arms and stepped onto the street to take him to the doctor's chamber, which was a stone's throw away from where we lived.

The doctor, a kind elderly gentleman, was surprised to see a patient so early in the morning and hurriedly opened the doors of his small chamber and let me in.

What followed was a routine check-up of the child as the doctor got busy with Rahul as he went over him minutely with his stethoscope while feeling the little one's pulse. He repeated his steps twice over, more slowly the next time around, as if affirming something to himself.

'Mr Dasgupta,' said the doctor, removing his reading glasses, as he handed over two vials of medicine. 'If I am not horribly wrong, I think I have heard a murmur in your child's heart.'

He then proceeded to explain, in the clearest terms possible, how the heart functioned and how he thought he had heard an abnormal murmur in the child's heart with all the potential signs that alluded either to a manageable case of a congenital heart defect or a heart valve disorder. He deduced this from the sound of the whoosh of the blood coursing through the heart.

I tried soaking in as much of the information as I could, and by the time the doctor was done, I had a bunch of questions for him.

Being a parent himself, the doctor understood the anxiety of a father and was patient throughout my long inquisition, assuring me of the well-being of my child, occasionally patting my hands, which helped a great deal to sooth my frayed nerves.

'Don't you worry, Mr Dasgupta,' he said, 'by the grace of God, your eldest has, I believe, a manageable form of the affliction. Simply put, the child would need careful nurturing and the strictest avoidance of anything strenuous.'

'I would strongly advise that the child be put through corrective surgery before he turns five to help him live a long and healthy life,' the doctor summed up, as he patted the papers on his table, signalling the end of the meeting.

As we stood in the doorway shaking hands, he patted my hand to reassure me and said, 'Just ensure that my recommendations are followed and things should be just fine in the interim.'

I came away from the doctor's chamber that morning with mixed emotions, feeling the full weight of responsibility that was now thrust upon my shoulders.

I was forever grateful to Dr Sarveshwar Rao for having pointed me to the right direction. But for him, we would have been in the dark for how long I dread to think.

With the twins now over three years old it was time, I thought, that we got Rahul through corrective surgery and most of the doctors whom I consulted in Calcutta concurred with my own intuitive assessment of the case.

With limited specialist hospitals available in Calcutta then, coupled with inordinately long waiting queues, we opted to take Rahul to the well-regarded Christian Medical College (CMC) in Vellore. Owned and administered by its administrative council made up of church leaders from across India, the hospital held the rare distinction of successfully performing India's first open-heart surgery in 1961 and following it up with India's first successful kidney transplant procedure in 1971.

I wanted nothing but the best for my child and India's best hospital bode well in my thoughts. Questions of affordability didn't faze me nor did my limited bank balance. Where other men would have weighed other options, my mind was fixated on my choice.

It was a formidable challenge to muster enough resources for a paediatric open-heart surgery within a limited time, but my pride kept me from asking people to help. I was determined to have it my way, but how?

It is always difficult to keep such things under wraps for long and it was not long before the grapevine at HCL got wind of my predicament and my steely resolve to get my son the best possible care in the land.

Suddenly, I found help streaming in from all quarters with my colleagues leading the charge. I remember a colleague who had made out a cheque for ₹1,000, a princely sum then, and had left it, exhibiting a great deal of sensitivity, on my table for me to find. I remember not mentioning a word to him on the subject when we next met—we just looked into each other's eyes, exchanging a subliminal message, as we stood shaking hands; he, I intuitively knew, would have been embarrassed by any other gesture.

There were him and countless others like him, including the likes of Shiv Nadar and Arjun Malhotra, who dipped into their own savings to help pull me out of my predicament and I couldn't thank them enough.

To me, the humanity and generosity shown by my colleagues was proof enough that behind the giant, seemingly impersonal machinery of the organisation, there are real people. It dawned on me that the machinery 'is' people, the sound of creaking wheels being actual live heartbeats throbbing through the organisation, and that lay at the heart of successful enterprises.

Five

Back from Vellore, I fell right back into the rough and tumble of life at HCL. Not that I sought any respite. We had built a formidable reputation and we intended sitting where we sat—at the top of the pile!

Having thrown open the doors of the primary market for us, Amit da, in his usual manner, agonised over putting a semblance of order and predictability into how the field made its sales call. It was all good to be cavalier and bloodthirsty, but with customers, too, wising up to the act, brute force could only take you so far.

It was Amit da who introduced us to the nuances of solution selling. Amit da toured around the country, personally training and mentoring us and the field guys. His travels would often bring him to Calcutta, from where it all started, to the delight of us—his most unabashed disciples.

An eloquent speaker and a passionate debater, I had first laid my eyes on Amit da when I had travelled to the Regional Engineering College at Durgapur to witness an intercollegiate debate competition featuring teams from some of the top colleges in east India. I remember that Amit da and his teammate, B.K. Singh, who later on went on to become the CEO of Brooke Bond, spoke passionately for the house and had the audience listening to them in rapt attention.

My memory fails whether Amit da and his mate went on to pick up the trophy of the day, but I distinctly remember walking away feeling delighted at having been privy to such a pair of erudite debaters.

A mentor's mentor, Amit da had his own affable way during his training sessions. His unyielding external visage hid a humorous core—a form of dry humour that tickled the intellect.

'So, I see,' he would say, pointing at one of the sales fellows, 'you have, as you have so correctly pointed out, latched on to that gold-laden rich seth in Chawri Bazaar,' all the while smiling as he peeked through his large immaculately clean glasses. 'But have you located the guy's hot button?'

The fellow would appear flummoxed for a while before quipping, 'I promise I will sell him two machines this month.'

He would then turn to me and Dadan Bhai and say, 'Look, here lies the issue...we are only pushing hardware where we should be pushing the rich, gold-laden seth, a solution...If you did that, he would be eating right out of your hands.'

It was from Amit da that we picked up the nuances of probing; asking customers all kinds of leading questions to identify their problem areas; issues that kept the fellow up at night. This we compiled and analysed and right enough we came up with the key pains ailing the customer— Amit da's 'hot button'.

Press the right 'hot button' and we had the customer in our bag. This practice also helped us a great deal in lucidly transmitting the customer's requirements to the solutions team to help design applications that worked for the customer. It was an amazing experience as we transited from being mere box-pushers to solution-providers.

Selling was not a gimmick or a sleight of hand as many made it out to be. To me, the act of selling was a pure religious activity and the best salesmen were the high priests in this temple. Amit da sat at the head of the table of high priests.

This is also to the credit of Amit da that he almost single-handedly managed to transform the work culture at HCL and in the process groomed his most devoted of disciples for life.

In time, as Amit da successfully navigated the marketing function, he and Arjun came to the conclusion that HCL was being severely bogged down by our method of one-to-one sales.

He, along with Arjun and Satrajit (Benu) Mazumdar, put their heads together and came up with the unique concept of 'roadshows' to help address large masses of customers within the confines of an environment that they were in control of.

It was thus they sought a meeting with Shiv and spread out before him the blueprint of their dream scheme. As Shiv pored over the plan,

Arjun explained the premise behind their thinking.

'So long, we have been used to selling one to one. We would need to change that to something like the predictability of a manufacturing process, you see,' he said, going on to add, 'something like having the customer go through a couple of stations, each priming him up for a buy, before we lead him to the cooking station for the final chop.'

HCL had a way with words and had developed its own unique lingo for almost anything. Thus was born the virulent terms 'slaughtering' and 'cooking'.

Brilliant in form and conception, the first 'pilot' roadshow was held at the Oberoi. The team took up the entire ground floor, the conference room and the function halls. Nothing less would have done. The senior team would then go from table to table as the sales team were in various stages of 'slaughtering' the prospects to finally guide the willing ones to the cooking platform where they were divested of their advance cheques—the final 'cooking' process. It was all great fun mixed with serious business.

The concept became so successful that it went on to become *the* most recognised way of selling, changing the face of how business was executed.

⁓

Six

WE WERE ALL CONSUMED by the new method of selling, coupled with our new-found ability to push solutions. Along with my team, I toured across large tracts of east India, taking our highly successful roadshow with us. We devised ingenious ways of avoiding paying octroi tax as we traversed state borders, at times lugging our heavy boxes of equipment over large distances.

In time, I was promoted up the chain and came to hold the position of regional sales manager (RSM) for east India. It was a period of great excitement and learning as I had to, for the first time, take responsibility for the entire revenue accruing from our part of the territory apart from expanding our base. We were growing at a phenomenal rate and there were times when the support and production guys struggled to keep pace with us.

As the RSM, I had to draw up budgets for the region's marketing and sales activities that were then normalised, keeping in view our yearly revenue projections that we broke down into quarters and months. The entire process of drawing up a budget was new to me and I found the experience greatly empowering. Ownership of revenue targets trebled when you knew that you had a highly vetted budget at your disposal.

The budget-making exercise helped spur the ability to think out of the box and to do more with less. There wasn't any fun if you got all that you wished for and this prodded you to devise ingenious schemes to get the maximum bang for the buck.

This reminds me of an incident that has remained forever etched in the annals of the great nuggets of learning that I have come across in my life.

We had returned from a successful roadshow to a neighbouring capital city and were thumping ourselves on the healthy order book that we had achieved from the trip, when, in the midst of our celebrations, I realised that we had overshot our budget for that particular roadshow by a couple of thousand bucks.

It didn't faze me since I had a healthy order book to show and promptly dashed off a note to the headquarters requesting sanctioning of the excess amount, which I wrote was a part of the 'business expenditure incurred towards the conduct of roadshow'.

It was not long before I got an equally brief note summoning me to New Delhi for a meeting with the chief Shiv Nadar himself.

'All for the sake of a couple of thousand bucks?' I thought, nodding, as I boarded the weekend train to Delhi. It puzzled me no end.

It was a sombre Shiv Nadar who sat opposite me during that meeting. Shiv was always sombre. To my theatrically bent mind, Shiv reminded me of the sages of yore, sitting still, deep in meditation and woe be to the one who shook them from their reverie. I hardly knew of anyone who did not dread those 'meetings' with him.

But here I was, after having had shaken Shiv from his reverie.

'Bikram,' he boomed from behind his bearded visage, 'I wanted to talk to you about two words in the English language.'

'One is termed as sanction and the other ratification. These are two very dissimilar words, Bikram,' he said, as his eyes bore into me. 'The word sanction, as you should know, always precedes the term ratification.' And with that, he pulled out the excess bill along with my neat handwritten note between us.

'What you are requesting me to do is to ratify the excess expenditure that you have incurred—money that is over and above the sanctioned amount,' he said as his fingers pointed to the offending figure in question.

'So, where will the money come from? Surely not from the company since it was neither sanctioned nor was permission sought.' And with that, he deftly signed off, approving my note.

'Be careful of those two words, Bikram,' Shiv said as he stood up, signalling the end of the meeting. 'Some day, you will lead your own company and people will be doing the same to you. How would you train them then?'

What an object lesson in taking financial responsibility and fiscal prudence, I thought, as I emerged from the meeting.

These two words have since been seared into my brain and one of the first things that I did, when I went to found my own company many years later, was to put in place a robust budgeting and sanctioning system.

♦

If we worked hard, we partied harder. There wasn't a reason we didn't party for. We celebrated our own achievements as much as we celebrated the achievements of the other regions and there was a great deal of bonhomie all around.

Vikram Hotel in New Delhi happened to be the team's favourite watering hole. Our meetings in New Delhi were packed days with sessions ranging from sales strategies, target setting to debating the next moves on the technology front. Nights were religiously crammed with serious partying sessions, some of which stretched till the wee hours of the morning. It was a great way to let our hair down as we drowned our woes in copious quantities of liquor.

Amit da was our favourite party guy and we all milled around him. He was among the rare few who could talk both about the French Revolution and IT in the same breath.

It was at one such do, after a long day of strenuous meetings, that Amit da, in his inimitable, understated style, plonked a large glass bowl in the middle of the throng saying, 'I don't want to hear one word about work or competition or technology. Just enjoy yourselves. Anyone defying my order will have to put ₹10 in the jar as a measure of atonement.'

Deed done, he disappeared to have a chat with Arjun who was standing, glass in hand, looking bemused as the entire event unfolded itself.

The party progressed somewhat more sedately when, suddenly, with some two or three pegs of drink sloshing around his belly, Rajiv Sahani, an ace salesman, who later on went on to become the UK head for HCL, stood up and looking at Amit da, pleaded, '*Hum ko bolne doh...mere se aur raha nahi ja raha hai* (I can't hold back any longer...please let me speak),' while dropping a ₹100 note into the empty glass bowl. And with that, he took off, true Delhi style, berating his competition, all the while peppering his talk with the choicest of Delhi's cuss words.

The bowl rapidly filled up with tenners as the guys merrily went back to what they did best—passionately discussing work, competitors and customers. This was the only time I had seen any of Amit da's schemes to fail so miserably.

∞

Seven

LIFE TRUDGED ON IN ITS usual hectic pace when one day, on returning from work, my eyes fell on a letter from Shuma lying on my table. She was not the writing kind, though we had kept in intermittent touch after I had shifted base to Calcutta.

I hoped that my premonition foretelling some foreboding news would be unfounded as I tore into the letter. She was writing from Delhi, where they had chosen to settle after Abhindra had returned from a six-month official sabbatical to Germany. Abhindra, she wrote, was extremely unwell and needed to undergo dialysis every day, leaving him weak and fatigued.

With a sinking feeling, I read on as she described how Abhindra had contracted SLE or Systemic Lupus Erythematosus, an autoimmune disease, during his trip to Germany; a syndrome where the body's immune system mistakenly attacks its own healthy tissue. SLE can affect the skin, joints, brain and other organs and in Abhindra's case, it was his kidneys.

Sleep was hard to come by that night and I caught the first available fast train to Delhi the next day. It was the springtime of 1983.

A distraught Shuma let me in. They didn't expect me to be at their door the next day and a restless Abhindra dragged himself out of his bed when he heard me talking to Shuma.

I was taken aback by how emasculated he looked and felt a flood of tears welling up. I struggled to hold them back as I embraced him in a big bear hug. For the first time in my life, I felt the god of words escape me as I felt his heart throb against mine.

Broken in body but not in spirit, Abhindra smiled warmly, his eyes brightened by the intellect of his soul, as he took me by my shoulders and led me to his bed. I sat him down, propped up by an army of pillows, as Shuma excused herself to drum up some food for the weary traveller, though I insisted that I had little appetite for food.

Abhindra would have none of it and looked on lovingly as I painfully dug into the food. 'I wish we could have done better, Bikram...' he said, letting the words trail off in the air.

That evening, we went for a long walk—not before I was satisfied that Abhindra had wrapped himself in a warm shawl. I didn't want him to catch a cold, given his hugely compromised immune system.

We walked as we had walked during our days at the IIT KGP campus. He took my hand as he narrated his ordeal, smiling all through. I remember that I hardly spoke, not wanting to break his train of thought, fearful of losing what he wanted to say.

'Bikram, it is all rotten luck that I have managed to contract SLE. I have dug through all the material that I could lay my hands on SLE and there is no cure for the guys eating into this fellow,' he said as he pointed to his kidneys.

'I am under the best possible care with the best doctors around me, but it would be tempting fate if I can last more than six months,' he said. 'Shuma knows this and I have been trying to convince her to get remarried when I am not around. She is too young to don a widow's attire and spend her life brooding. Her best years are still ahead of her.'

'It is my fervent wish,' he said, looking at me, 'that Shuma gets remarried and follows none of the restrictions that widowhood so unkindly bequeaths upon our womenfolk.'

'This, Bikram,' he said as he took my hands into his, 'is what we call fate—Karma is a better word; we must accept "it" as "it" is. The earlier you accept it the better it is for everyone. You are then at peace with yourself and the world.

I didn't know what to make of Abhindra's cheerfulness and his imperturbable acceptance for what fate, or karma in his words, had laid out for him. I couldn't feel as stoic as he did, try as I might, and returned home enveloped in a deep and lingering sadness.

I made it a point to visit Abhindra every other week. I would catch the Saturday train to Delhi, arrive on Sunday, spend the day with him and catch the night train back to Calcutta.

I was at work one day, some five months after I had first met the ailing Abhindra, when Ranjana called me, informing that he had passed away.

I sat, numbed, at my desk before I managed to pick myself up. I rushed home to pick up a change of clothes before heading to the airport and caught the first available flight to Delhi.

I landed at the Delhi airport cursing the vagaries of Indian Airlines, the only carrier in those days. The family had already taken the body to the cremation grounds by the time I had managed to dash across to Abhindra's home.

I made the journey back to Calcutta clinging to the urn that contained Abhindra's ashes. To me, that was Abhindra.

Over time, we had Shuma shift to Calcutta along with her young son and settled her in a house in AD Block in Salt Lake, a few blocks away from our house in AE Block.

Ranjana and I made it a point to visit Shuma almost every day to give her the companionship that she needed during those days and it cheered her. Gradually, as she came around to accept Abhindra's absence, we started taking her out to movies and shopping arcades, trying our best to integrate her back to the normal humdrum of life.

Another of Abhindra's close friends, Dr Subir Choudhury, whom we knew as Laltu, an alumnus of Jadavpur University, played a yeoman's role in helping rehabilitate Shuma. Abhindra had come to know Laltu from his DRDO days and both of them were an integral part of *Aachal Adhuli Gosthi*, an amateur theatre group that specialised in staging one-act plays.

A few years later, Shuma came to meet a gentleman some three batches senior to us at IIT KGP, who was also a widower. He had unfortunately lost his wife in an accidental kitchen fire, leaving behind a small boy. In him, Shuma found a kindred soul and over time, as they came to know each other better, decided to tie the knot and settle down in Calcutta.

I was happy in Shuma's happiness and I thought that was what Abhindra would have wanted too. I could well imagine a smiling and happy Abhindra, looking down from the sky, to see a settled and secure Shuma.

Eight

IT WAS IN MID-1983 WHEN Dadan Bhai chose to give up his job at HCL to chase his own entrepreneurial dreams. He shifted base to Delhi and set up Altos India Ltd. Altos began operations by tapping into the still nascent gaming console market, something that Dadan Bhai believed would be the next game-changer. He was right, but was off by many a decade.

His absence left a void in the eastern India operations as I gingerly stepped into his large shoes as the acting regional manager as the management scouted for a more veteran profile to helm the operations. In time, they appointed A.K. Basu, the regional customer engineering manager, as the regional manager (East), though I still called the operational shots.

There weren't too many days during my life at HCL where I didn't learn something new and which didn't leave an imprint on my life. The arc of learning spread pretty wide, starting off from learning to sell, marketing, people management, strategy and planning, to hard-nosed execution.

Of all the things that HCL did, it taught me to think big. Nothing was too big or too audacious. If it was, it was only in one's mind. There was no barrier that was insurmountable and no challenge insoluble.

The naked flaunting of an overarching ambition and unfettered aspiration broke me away from my middle-class fetters of thinking small and in manageable chunks.

The great thing about it all was that learning came from people of all hues and shapes—ranging from the sombre Shiv, to the gentle giant Arjun, to the literary and marketing guru Amit da, to the rustic genius in Dadan Bhai.

Rajendra S. Pawar (or Raji as he was more popularly known) was a great example in edifying how one approached one's work with the seriousness of purpose that it deserved. This being said, he too, had that audacious streak in him that marked out every one of us.

It reminds me of being on a joint call with him to the Durgapur steel plant. Raji was then the corporate planning manager and head of HCL's newest offering—the System 4, a 16-bit computer based on the latest bit-slice architecture. For the uninitiated, this architecture was especially used for microprocessors in which the CPU, the central processing unit, was fabricated by concatenating a number of high-performance processing units or 'slices'. Each of these 'slices' represented a limited width (8 bits in our case) of an ALU, arithmetic logic unit, and CU, the control unit, section.

I had set up a meeting with Mr Tarafdar, the head of systems, as we were fighting against a competing product from DCM Data Systems. Our System 4 had been tentatively priced at a princely sum of ₹16 lakh. The product had yet to reach the prototyping phase, but true to style, HCL had gone ahead with launching the product with a series of adverts promising delivery in four weeks.

It was thus that we met Mr Tarafdar, Raji beaming with confidence about his new product—which was not a surprise to me, well-versed as I was in HCL's guerilla marketing tactics.

Raji presented a fascinating picture during such client calls. Introductions dispensed with, Raji would proceed by neatly placing his large top zip briefcase against the chair, as he took his seat, and go on to take off his wristwatch, which he noiselessly placed on the table, the dial facing him. With the client looking on, Raji would then proceed to open his briefcase and produce a largish writing pad and begin his sales pitch in right earnest.

As he spoke, he would pause ever so often to write on his pad exactly what he spoke and also recorded the customer's voice. To the customer, it all seemed extremely academic and highly erudite. Never had the fellow come across a gentleman who wrote as he spoke and seemed to cling onto every word that transpired between them. To Raji, it was a part of his regimented sales practice and was not a show to be put on.

As this went on, Raji would suddenly turn to me, stopping the customer dead on his tracks, and say, 'What time did you say my train is, Bikram? We can't afford to get delayed, can we?' smiling at Mr Tarafdar, who by now had fallen for Raji's charm and didn't feel a whiff of the hustling that was going on.

Mr Tarafdar, somewhat convinced that the product met all his requirements and more, felt that he needed some more material evidence on the product. Looking at Raji, he said, 'I am convinced of the product, but since we are buying such an expensive product, the least we could do is see a photograph of the machine.'

'Now what?' I thought as Raji dipped right into his briefcase and fished out a photograph of an old IBM machine with no resemblance with the still-to-be-born System 4 and held the photograph up for a nanosecond, saying, 'If I told you this is what System 4 would look like, would it have made any difference?' before dropping it right into the briefcase.

Looking seriously at Mr Tarafdar, he said 'We will await your visit to Delhi and we really look forward to demonstrating the machine, but I understand that you have your process to follow and since I have to leave, my young colleague here, Mr Dasgupta, will help you with all the formalities to prepare for the visit and the order.' And with that, Raji strapped his wristwatch back, signalling the end of the meeting.

The same Rajendra Pawar, whom I had never seen to be attired in anything but a dark coat matched with dark blue trousers, chose to transform his looks, letting go of the coat and opting for khadi shirts when he went on to co-found the National Institute of Information Technology (NIIT), immersing himself in his new role as an educationist. This was the religiosity with which the early stalwarts took their roles in life.

The guys on the frontline were no different either when it came to holding the torch aloft.

I thrived in their company—from Rajiv Sahni to Satrajit (Benu) Mazumdar, who held the unique distinction of convincing a client to buy an annual maintenance contract a full quarter before he bought the machine, to Manpreet Singh, who didn't think twice of charming an influential client's wife, helping her chop vegetables for the evening meal, all for the sake of bagging an order.

This was all to change when I got a call from Dadan Bhai one evening as I was getting ready to leave office, the voice at the other end of the line booming: 'Dasgupta Seth, I have some serious talking to do...let's have dinner together.'

Nine

I MET DADAN BHAI AT THE Oberoi Grand as he sat at the restaurant humming to himself, half his shirt buttons open. This was typical of Dadan Bhai, who didn't give a damn about what others thought of him as he lounged within the pristine environs of the five-star hotel, a story in disarray, his hair hurriedly patted into place.

As we sat nursing our drinks, Dadan Bhai was a picture of composure, but I could feel a storm raging within him. We chatted about his latest venture, Altos, as he brought me up to speed with the gaming market in India—still an aspirational product with a limited customer base.

You could tell when Dadan Bhai was on a hunt as he was that evening. An extremely sharp fellow, he would spring for the kill when you least expected, but till then he would be laser-focused on his prey, and veer all discussions around to suit his ultimate agenda. I have never seen a person more focused or steely minded to achieve what he set out for.

As we went through dinner, Dadan Bhai suddenly stopped eating and said in a voice that brooked no dissent, 'Tell Babli (he always called my wife by her nickname) that you are with Dadan Bhai and won't be returning home tonight.' And with that, he merrily tucked back hungrily into his food.

Dadan Bhai had, with great foresight and planning, booked a twin bedded room (his planning was always meticulous when it came to stalking his quarry) and we settled in for the night. We discussed his dreams and aspirations—his need to grow big, the need to build an organisation that would be rivalled by none in the country. He moaned about how he knew all about finances but fell short when it came to marketing finesse or handling the manufacturing part of his operations.

It was not before long that he let go of his golden arrow from his armoury. 'I need you Dasgupta Seth,' he said in characteristic Dadan-speak. 'No one but you can handle marketing. *Angrezi bol ne wala bhi toh chahiye* (English speakers are also needed). Come to think of it, there is none other than you who would fit the role. I am convinced of it and I will not have it any other way.'

No one understood me as well as perhaps Dadan Bhai did. His '*Angrezi bol ne wala bhi toh chahiye*' was his own euphemism for recognising the skills that I had and the potential that he saw in me.

It was during that fateful night that we gave birth to PCL (Pertech Computers Ltd) in our dreams, and boy, did we think big! We let the horses loose from their stables as we discussed through the better part of the night, sleeping only for a few hours in the wee hours of the morning.

Dadan Bhai was relentless and dogged in his pursuit and would not rest until he had checked all the boxes in his agenda. He pushed, bullied and pleaded till we agreed upon my gradual disengagement from HCL and shifting base to Delhi, our first expansion plans and the rough contours of our newly minted business plan.

In the meantime, Dadan Bhai had done his groundwork well. It was through the HCL grapevine that I had learnt that he had, in the preceding five months, managed to magically rope in Arjun Malhotra as his sleeping partner in Altos, along with Bharat Goenka, an IIT Kanpur alumnus whose elder brother, Bijoy Goenka, was Dadan's classmate at IIT.

It was a much calmer Dadan Bhai that I met in the morning, part of his storm abated. He had neatly netted his fish, both with vaulting dreams and parting with a slice of the new company. He now had in place the first of his active stakeholders with whom he could dream along.

I believe Dadan put on the same roadshow as he scoured the country in his quest to have the best people for our new organisation. In the end, he ended up netting all those he had targeted for his ambitious plans.

Altos was to later transform into the manufacturing arm for PCL, PCL being the marketing arm of the venture.

Back at HCL, life continued at its hectic pace. With Dadan Bhai doing the vanishing act, it largely fell upon me to keep the flag flying at full mast.

Dadan had chosen his time well to don his running shoes. Between the two of us and the team, we had managed to pull up the eastern region to the No. 1 slot among all regions based on sales volumes, and Dadan, always the poster boy, was posted to Delhi for more important things. Not the one to give up on this opening, he put his time and networking skills into play to create Altos, which subsequently went on to become the backbone of our engineering and manufacturing functions.

Dadan Bhai had left me in a great quandary. Here I was, scarcely three years into HCL, finding myself staring at an unknown angel again. I knew both Arjun and Amit da loved me dearly and that they had pegged high hopes on me. I could foresee with a certain degree of certainty the future that HCL held for me and besides, the great ecosystem of learning at HCL pulled at my heartstrings.

As I thought more and more on the subject, I got increasingly convinced that the unknown held far greater rewards than the known. Sure, the risks were far greater and the stakes much higher than when I had decided to part ways with Indian Oxygen, but I also knew myself. I knew deep down that I wouldn't be able to forgive myself if I chose a path that was easy—a path that offered the least resistance. I would be better treading on stones and following my intuitive instincts than having it any other way.

Meanwhile, those at the upper echelons of HCL realised that they ran the risk of losing me to competition if they were to keep me in Calcutta under A.K. Basu, the regional manager. Not that Basu was a bad manager, but he was too docile and sedate for a young gun like me who loved the rush of a battle and the smell of gunpowder in his nostrils.

Fortuitously for me, HCL had me transplanted to Delhi as the business development manager for HCL's foray into direct retailing in the form of Computer Shoppe. Reporting directly to Shiv Nadar himself, it suited me well since I had already firmed up my mind to work with Dadan Bhai.

While it may sound opportunistic to some, to me it was fate that was pulling me towards a pre-defined destiny. I didn't quite put it in those exact words then, but I did feel that the puzzle pieces were nicely falling into their slots—thank you!

If working with Dadan Bhai was a baptism by fire, my short stint with Shiv Nadar exposed me to an entirely different style of management. Where Dadan Bhai was purely result driven and would care less if you followed any process or not, Shiv Nadar stood out in sharp contrast.

A man of very few words, he insisted on method and form as the best possible way to achieve the desired outcome. To him, structure and processes were paramount and he relentlessly pursued the same. In this, he stood out from his contemporaries like Arjun Malhotra. To Shiv, business growth came by following a strictly regimented and structured path where emotions or raw passion had little or no role to play.

A master strategist, I often found Shiv thinking aloud 'what next' and 'how next'. He was forever pushing the boundaries and prodding into the darkness of the unknown, a behavioural facet that I found intriguing and was felt drawn by the charm of it.

Shiv was a great devotee of the top-down management style and was somewhat vertically focused in his functioning. This very much suited the HCL of those days. His approach ensured that each of us were clearly aligned with the goals and expectations of the corporation and gave persons, up and down the chain, more time to focus on the task at hand rather than waste valuable time debating potential directions for the company. It also helped immensely in bestowing upon HCL the drive that its competitors so sorely lacked.

In about a month into my posting in Delhi, I walked into Sujit Bakshi's office to tender my resignation. Sujit, who headed the HR function, appeared fazed by my decision, but being the astute man manager that he was, he left it to me to take the path that best suited my instincts. I, on my part, assured him that I wasn't leaving HCL to join another company but was joining hands with Dadan Bhai to whet my entrepreneurial urge.

There was no subterfuge in our dealings then and we were unafraid of talking our minds, man-to-man as it were, without fear of favour or reprisals. This is something that I find awfully lacking these days. I find it difficult to fathom why a young, or for that matter any employee, would put on such elaborate ruses to conceal where one is moving to.

With Sujit, I did speak my mind. We agreed on a six-month transition period, which I was to later extend to nine months on HCL's request, where I could be allowed to be on leave for extended lengths of time to help set up my new venture while ensuring a smooth transition at HCL. Sujit readily agreed to my proposition and I felt as if a weight had been lifted off my shoulders.

Expectedly, it didn't take long for the news of my resignation to reach Shiv Nadar and the rest of his mates. Shiv justifiably was taken aback and very upset. He had started liking me, calling me an 'ideas' man and I guess he was loath to lose a resource that HCL had readily invested itself in. He must have also realised that with Dadan and me coming together, another unwarranted competitor was in the making.

It was a mighty upset Shiv that took Arjun aside and swearing on their friendship told him, 'Whatever you have to do with Dadan and Altos you do, I will not come in between, but Bikram isn't going anywhere.'

Knowing Arjun and the genial giant that he was, and is, he must have been put in an immensely awkward position. Arjun always chose to follow his heart and to him friendship stood above anything and here he was, the poor fellow, torn between his friendship for Shiv and Dadan. It must have been with a great deal of trepidation that he decided to put his weight behind Shiv's decision.

It had been less than a week since I had put in my papers when I heard the doorbell at my C.R. Park residence ringing loudly. It was well past midnight in the Delhi winter. I hurriedly undid the locks, pondering who could be at the door at such an unearthly hour and dreaded some awful news when I saw a harried Sujit standing by the collapsible door grill.

'What brings you here at this hour, Sujit?' I asked him, as I started parting the grill. 'Come on in.'

'Don't bother with the grill, Bikram. I am good standing here,' he said. 'I have come here not as the HR head of HCL but as a friend—to meet a friend whom I love dearly.'

'That's all good, but why won't you come in?' I asked.

'I won't, now listen to me, Bikram, but before that fetch two glasses, will you?'

I felt intrigued by Sujit's behaviour but chose to keep my wisdom to myself and scurried off to fetch the glasses.

I handed him the two glasses in turns as Sujit poured two healthy shots of rum from his cask and gulped it down in one shot, his face turning red in the cold Delhi winter.

'Better, now getting to the point, the upper floor guys at HCL have taken a decision to not let go of you, Bikram, and it comes from right at the top,' he said in Bengali.

I looked at his flushed face and said, 'What! I am all set to go, Sujit. My bags are packed and ready. Tell me you are not being serious!'

'I am being dead serious, Bikram. What else would have prodded me to leave my warm bed at this unholy hour and have you ram open your doors,' and went on to tell me what had transpired between Shiv and Arjun.

'Well,' I said, putting in an effort to keep my composure and sound jovial, 'if this is a joke, it is well taken and you did pull one, I would say!'

Sujit still had that deadpan look about him as he pleaded, 'I leave it up to you to take this seriously or not, Bikram. I did what I felt a friend should do. But you should ponder over it...it's your career that we are talking about here.'

Ranjana had, in the meantime, stood by the stairs and had been privy to our midnight tryst. We spent the better part of the night discussing what might happen. Knowing Shiv, I knew how serious he was about this issue and wouldn't be the one to lay his arms down so easily.

Still unsure of what to do and what turn events might take, I waited till the first rays of light broke through the drapes before placing a call to Dadan Bhai. There wasn't Dadan Bhai's familiar 'Dasgupta Seth' floating through the lines and in its stead a sleepy gruff voice told me that 'Sahib is out on a tour.'

Not knowing what to do, I decided to meet Dadan's wife Chitra, whom I knew well, to share my predicament. There was no one else whom I could run to for succour.

'What a mess,' I chided myself as I climbed up the stairs to Chitra's office at the Bank of India. Chitra was surprised to see me at her office and coming up to me said, '*Kya hua*, Bikram? What brings you all the way here to my office?'

'Can we step aside, please,' I pleaded. 'It is very important that I talk to you.'

Chitra patiently heard out the entire story before saying, 'Well, there is nothing that we can do now, but Dadan would be back by the evening flight. Let's both go to the airport and meet him.'

'Come on, Chitra,' I chided her, 'why are you playing with me, this is serious.'

'I am serious, Bikram. There is no harm in going to the airport and meeting Dadan, is there?' she said and smiling mischievously added, 'I will get to know my real Dadan by seeing how he reacts when you tell him this. You stay up in the front and I will trail you.'

We met Dadan at the airport that evening. Dadan was his usual self—half his shirt buttons open and hurriedly patted down hair (I have never had the privilege of ever seeing him make use of a comb to tame his unruly mop!), humming to himself as he exited the airport.

He spied me waiting for him and came up saying, '*Arre* Dasgupta Seth, *aap* airport *mein, kya hua?* (What brings you to the airport?)'

I took him aside and for the second time in the day narrated what had transpired between Sujit Bakshi and me.

No sooner had he heard me out than he started guffawing. He took me by my shoulders and said, 'Dasgupta Seth, you and I have decided to work together, you and I will work together, and merry be to the world that would like to think otherwise...' a few of his choicest cuss words dangling dangerously in thin air as he held them back.

'What a waste of time,' he said as he disappeared laughing into his car, a smiling Chitra in tow.

❧

Rajasthan, a border state on the western fringes of India, has always been a land fiercely proud of its independence. By the 16th century, its frontiers were being slowly eroded from the pressure exerted by the marauding Mughal warriors who ruled vast tracts of India from Delhi.

In the midst of this crisis arose a hero from the dunes of Rajasthan to rally its people under his banner. Endowed with an indomitable spirit, Rana Pratap was a formidable warrior and thought nothing of facing up to his biggest enemy—Akbar, the great Mughal emperor. Rana Pratap remains a revered name in modern India.

This is how I would like to introduce Bikram Dasgupta. He never shied away from action and was single-handedly responsible, with limited resources at his command, for the PCL–Dell joint venture in India. It was one of the first such partnerships in the Indian information technology industry and his setting up of the export division was another great achievement.

I would consider BDG as the shining star of the IT industry of his era.

Ashwini Talwar
(Former executive director of PCL,
Ashwini worked with Bikram during his PCL days)

Ten

I JOINED PCL AS ONE OF ITS CO-FOUNDERS in early 1984 for what would prove to be a long and tumultuous journey. For the first time, I was free from the fetters that tied me down as an employed professional and had embarked upon what was to be my everlasting tryst with entrepreneurship.

I was a first-generation entrepreneur and felt proud of it, being the only one in my family to break the shackles of a staid and predictable life. It suited my temperament immensely and I thrived in its limelight.

One of the first things that we did on joining PCL was to ease the company out of the gaming hardware business. Dadan had also come to realise that it was going nowhere and readily acquiesced to focusing our energies on reinventing ourselves.

Meanwhile, Dadan had managed to rope in some of the brightest minds of the day for PCL. Anil Bhushan Chopra, an ace computer salesman, was roped in to head the sales division, while I straddled the marketing and strategy functions. Anil, whom we jocularly called the ABC of computer selling (the first letters of his name fitting in beautifully), had built a fearsome reputation for himself at HCL. The first to finish his monthly targets, he could invariably be spied, for the better part of a month, lounging at one of the swimming pools of a five-star hotel, a beer bottle astride his chest, all because he had nothing to do, having executed whatever target was given to him. He swatted targets as one swatted flies.

Dadan had planned his moves well; PCL got its ruggedness from Anil and polish from me, and what a combination it proved to be!

For the Research and Development (R&D) division, Dadan managed to cajole A.S. Mittal, another of HCL's bright brains, whom he paired with Stephen Aranha, an IIT Madras and IIM Calcutta alumnus, again poached from HCL's rich stables, to head his engineering and production functions.

Each one of us were handed dreams, a slice of the new company and a free rein to build the organisation of our dreams, while Dadan took charge of managing our banking function, raising money and keeping an eye on the finances of the fledgling company.

With the team in place, we decided to get off the ground by marketing electronic typewriters, which were in essence dedicated word processors, some sporting multiline Cathode Ray Tube (CRT) displays and came with rudimentary spellcheckers.

Straddling between a regular (dumb) typewriter and a much smarter, but costlier computer, electronic typewriters had caught the fancy of business establishments and held out a lot of promise. With not too many competitors around, low market entry barriers and a much faster sales cycle, we decided to sell Japan's Brother electronic typewriters.

Armed with the knowledge that Brother wouldn't bother to hand over any sort of territorial distributorship rights to a fledgling company, we decided to chuck the rule book and instead got in touch with one of the largest importers of Brother machines in India.

Forever the consummate dealmaker, Dadan convinced the owner-manager of the firm to import electronic typewriters in lots of hundreds, which he promised to push out to the market at the fastest possible pace provided he stored the imports at his warehouses. To cap it all, PCL promised to pay the importer in full once a sale was closed.

Armed with this lopsided deal under his arm, the chairman of PCL chose to stride into his office at S-137, Greater Kailash-I, New Delhi, humming more cheerily than other days, shirt buttons open halfway— and thus started our journey in right earnest.

The only vexing question remaining on the table was the mechanics of tapping into the vast market opportunity that the entire landmass of India promised. Where others would have started small, taking one chunk of the country at a time, Dadan would have none of it. We had to attack on all fronts simultaneously if we had to keep our date with the aggressive sales forecasts.

Dadan took the southern and eastern territories, while I volunteered for the western half of the country. Anil took up the remaining northern territory with Stephen and Mittal, the poor chaps, setting up their repair shop in one of the unused toilets of the office—refurbished to erase any traces of its previously inglorious past.

With my family and twins settled in Delhi, I packed my bags for Bombay. For the next three years, it became a ritual for me to fly back to Delhi during the weekends and holidays to catch up with my rapidly growing twins and the family. It was perhaps the most hectic phase of my life.

Arriving in Bombay, a city that I had never been to before, I was struck by the cosmopolitan air of its denizens and its gushing crowds that seemed to appear from every nook and cranny of the city. It was a city that was perennially in a rush and the jam-packed suburban train system—the lifeline of the city—was a sight to behold.

It took me a while to get used to the crowds and the art of managing a toehold in the morning rush hour train that somehow seemed to defy the laws of physics in its capacity to hold so many heaving bodies in a constrained space. To my amazement, the carriages never seemed to mind the weight as they merrily criss-crossed across the weaving lines, disgorging and engorging itself at each stop on its route.

We still didn't have a proper office in Bombay. We couldn't afford one and had to make do with a small space that we co-shared with one of our larger distributors for what seemed to be a princely sum of money. Meetings at that office were out of question and I chose to call the team manning the Bombay office, to my hotel for our maiden meeting.

There were a total of eight or nine young fellows led by a senior sales executive running the show. No sooner had I started the meeting, the guys having had a round of tea to shake off their travel weariness, that they started coming up to me and handed in their resignation letters.

I could sense that it was premeditated move but couldn't fathom what had caused such a mutiny in the ranks. I waited for the dust to settle down before asking them what had caused this sudden change of heart.

It was the fustiest of rehearsed speeches that I heard from the ringleader—the senior sales executive. He said that they, as a group, felt that the company had no future and it would go nowhere with its current plans (how were they privy to our plans, I wondered) and that they wouldn't like to jeopardise their own careers by staying with such an organisation.

Having delivered his monologue, the ringleader looked around at his mates as they dutifully nodded their heads, agreeing to all that was said.

'Well,' I said in a warm voice, 'since it seems that all of you have already made up your minds, I can't do much about it except wishing you the very best for your future journey and careers, but I have only one request. Give me just 90 days to prove what we can achieve together and if you still find what the gentleman had earlier said to be true, I will accept your resignations. Till then, I will retain your papers with me.'

There were some back and forth before the guys reluctantly decided to put in their lot with me; some of them though, I must admit, weren't taken in by my plan.

I let go of the ringleader some months down the line, but a majority of the guys who had assembled in that small hotel room that day ended up spending more than a decade with PCL, witnessing its most momentous days. Most of them went on to join some of the most admired companies in the world and among them was Karun Rishi, a Delhi boy, who emerged as one of my best salesmen in PCL.

With almost no office to speak of, we made the parks and beaches of Bombay our meeting grounds. We discussed sales strategies, chased up targets, held review meetings and pursued outstandings, armed with packets of warm peanuts. Any sales closure called for instant beer parties and bigger deals meant some serious whisky drinking.

Western India proved to be a happy hunting ground, the businessmen more astute than their counterparts in other parts of the country. Not having a regular office carried its own perks as we hopped between locations, changing our scenery frequently, helping keep our batteries charged. It was a time of great fun and youthful energy.

❧

Eleven

IN HINDSIGHT, THE DECISION TO hawk Brother's electronic typewriters proved to be a brilliant one. The only other competitor worthy of mention was HCL's Network Ltd, which sold the Swedish Hermes electronic typewriters. These were bulky and somewhat ugly machines.

In contrast, Brother electronic typewriters stood out by their sleek design. It had a small form factor and we got the ones that came in all black with smart green keys. The customers loved the design and since it came with Japanese credentials, they had enough confidence in the performance and durability of the machines.

Over a period of time, with stocks flying rapidly off the shelves, we upped the game with our distributor and had him ship in typewriters in lots of 200–300 machines. It was always a cash flow game, subsisting as we were on the margins that we made, hanging by the credit thread extended by our benevolent importer-agent.

We lived dangerously and took the kind of risks that surprises me today. Not to be found lacking in marketing firepower, while fully in the know that we had no formal arrangements with Brother, we went on to invest in large newspaper advertisements proclaiming the merits of Brother electronic typewriters, printing Brother's logo in sizes that were hard to miss.

We did ask ourselves what our reactions would be if those adverts came to Brother's notice, but failing to dig up any suitable response that might assuage the corporation's ego, decided to banish such thoughts forever. The warrior in Dadan Bhai loved it all and hugged me in a bear embrace when I told him that 'we shall cross the bridge once we come upon it'. So, the water kept flowing and orders poured in from all over the country.

Into my second stint of virtual bachelorhood in Bombay, I had put up with a well-to-do Sindhi family at Cuffe Parade, now transformed into an upmarket neighbourhood, in South Mumbai.

It still manages to bring a smile to my face, recalling the lengths that the family patriarch, an educated businessman, went on to shield his teenage daughter from my gaze.

Forever in the dread that his daughter would fall for the handsome Bengali or vice versa, no matter of protestations or telling him that I was a happily married man, with two growing twins, nothing would assuage the father's anxiety.

◆

With a rapidly mounting top-line, we decided that it was time to make a serious try at formalising our relationship with Brother. Nothing less than a national distributorship would do and that in itself posed a formidable challenge, let alone our complete ignorance of the Japanese psyche.

It was important that we arrived at some form of arrangement with Brother and the criticality of the meeting was not lost upon us. Even the ever effervescent Dadan Bhai quit his humming during the long 12-hour flight to Tokyo.

Having had never negotiated with Japanese professionals before, we didn't know quite what to expect. The only nuggets of information that we could glean came from the importer who shipped us the Brother machines.

'The Japanese are a quiet bunch,' he had warned, 'and they don't take kindly to any sort of hustling, so keep off it.' He knew Dadan and me well enough to ward us off from our battle tactics. 'These guys love to take their time and no amount of throwing numbers at them will help… so keep your patience and be nice guys,' he said, as he walked us to the door wishing us luck in our venture. He also armed us with a letter highly recommending us and spoke quite eloquently of our marketing muscle.

We got off at Narita (Tokyo) International Airport to be greeted by sleets of rain and a dark grey sky. The cold nip in the air did nothing to lift our sombre mood as we made our way to Shinjuku station to catch a bus to Nagoya—the cheapest mode of transport available for budget travellers like us.

It was nightfall by the time we made our way to one of Nagoya's budget hotels and crashed out. The twelve-hour flight with an eight-hour bus ride thrown in had drained us of our energies. We had a miserable Japanese meal, unaccustomed as we were to the food of the land, and I soon found myself dreaming of a piping hot homemade meal.

We woke up in the morning to a happily humming Dadan Bhai lighting into what seemed his fourth cigarette since the morning—he was a serious chain-smoker. His yesterday's solemn mood washed away by a healthy bout of sleeping, he looked at peace with himself with not a care for the burden that we shouldered.

'Good morning, Dasgupta Seth,' he chimed in sweetly. 'Go on, have a bath in Nagoya,' he said in his Bhojpuri-laced Hindi, rhyming Nagoya with the Hindi word for naked, laughing loudly at his joke. Sharp and witty, Dadan Bhai was the only one in his family to see the insides of an IIT and had managed to graduate at the age of 16 when most people would have just managed to pass out of school.

We decided to leave our adventure with Japanese cuisine for later in the trip and instead opted for omelettes—the safest option that we could glean from the menu.

A twenty-minute taxi ride later brought us to Naeshiro-cho, Mizuho-ku in the Aichi prefecture—the headquarters of Brother. Housed in an imposing six-storeyed complex in white, with glass cladding all round, we were inundated with a mass of signage in Japanese as we made our way to the reception.

The petite receptionist manning a bank of imposing-looking phones didn't quite know what to make out of the three brown travellers that presented themselves before her that morning. Her halting English, which promised to fall apart at the next bend, only flustered her more till she happened to come upon one of the office staff on his coffee run. Excusing herself with a deep bow, she spoke to the guy in rapid-fire Japanese and had him scurrying in the opposite direction, stranding his coffee with the lady.

She bowed deeply again and we awkwardly followed suit as she stepped out from behind her imposing desk and led us to the sitting area.

With her travellers settled, she rapidly shuffled away only to disappear behind the safety of her desk.

We didn't have to wait long before a gentleman presented himself before us and we stood to greet him as he bowed deeply to us. We followed suit and shook hands. The guy thankfully knew enough English to let us know that he was from the international sales division and that we were welcome to Brother.

We, in turn, spoke rather slowly and told him that we were from India before Dadan helpfully chirped in with 'we are the largest electronic typewriter selling company in India' as we looked on incredulously.

The unfazed Japanese executive rapidly twitched his eyebrows, never ever having heard the name PCL before, but kept his composure and led us to a long conference room only to shuffle out again, this time to call his boss.

The young executive returned in a while with what seemed to be his boss, a weather-beaten gentleman in the mid-40s, with two more of his colleagues, both younger to him by many years.

Introductions and a lot of bowing later, we settled down for what turned out to be a fairly long meeting. The boss man heard us patiently as we described to him our operations, with many offices strewn across India (we merrily added to the numbers), and how we had perfected the art of selling Brother machines.

The boss man didn't smile nor let his eyes belie his thoughts. He excused himself as he turned to his yearlings and, as we were intended to believe, explained the purport of our monologue. The guys intoned 'hai' ever so often, followed by a vigorous nodding of their heads, as the boss man fired away, that it led us to believe that we had done a good job.

Turning his attention to us, the boss man spoke in surprisingly good English, and said that he was aware of the Indian market and that he had been to India once before but had returned rather disappointed. It sank our hearts to hear that.

'Indian love Amrican. I see lots of Amrican electronics. Very few Japanese, except camera...'

We were at a loss for words and even Dadan Bhai kept quiet before I told our deadpan boss man names of some of the largest outfits in India that were using Brother and other Japanese products. Thankfully, the guy didn't prod further and ask about the other Japanese products in use.

'Well,' he said, 'but do you know anything about electronics and typewriters? Brother Electronics is very advanced.'

As we looked at each other trying to form a response, Stephen Aranha, who had been a quiet observer for so long, requested the boss man for the latest model of their typewriter along with a tool set.

This caught the boss man by surprise and somewhat intrigued, ran one of his subordinates down for the stuff that Stephen had asked for.

With the typewriter rested on a non-static mat, Stephen proceeded to delicately undo the machine. He went in like a surgeon, his hands and fingers working deftly as he dug into the machine, neatly disembowelling its parts and laying them on the mat. What was a fully assembled printer a few minutes back looked a hollow shell by the time he was the done.

With the Japanese eagerly looking on, Stephen went about meticulously stitching his patient back and had the printer reassembled in some 15-odd minutes. With the flourish of a maestro, he plugged the machine into the wall socket and switched it on—and on it came in all its glory, the indicator lights happily switching on as the fluorescent display turned bright and green.

For the first time during our meeting we saw the boss man breaking into a small smile. The Japanese respected competence and workmanship and Stephen had proved it to them on their own turf. He had single-handedly pushed us several notches up the ladder.

Back in India, armed with the distribution agreement with Brother, there was no stopping us. The first thing we did was to release a full-page ad in all national dailies; the headline screamed 'Japan's No. 1 Company joins hands with India's No. 1 Company' followed by a fierce-looking crouching sumo wrestler. This time, we printed the Brother logo in an even bigger size.

We immediately found ourselves in the midst of a minor scrape with Brother—they didn't quite take to our aggressive stance and let us know in so many words. I remember that we brazened through it with a lot of cheek and some sweet talking.

We happily took the Brother machines to most of the industrial exhibitions and ended up earning some massive brownie points against our rivals. In one such exhibition, we had some Network guys leering at our dainty little machines when I overheard one of them quipping, 'Is that a toy?'

'Yes,' I said, as I patted one of our machines. 'You are right. It might look like a toy, but be careful, the bite is sharp!' sending them slithering away to their stall.

♾

Your curiosity, mischievousness and *joie de vivre* have always made you stand apart from others. Your ability to find excitement in things others find normal has surely contributed to your great success.

Entrepreneurs thrive on the potent combination of unquenchable curiosity, a deep and abundant source of energy, a penchant for making friends so easily, and the raw power of intellect. I have always enjoyed your company because you are a storehouse of all these qualities.

Rajendra S. Pawar (Raji)
(Padma Bhushan awardee; former chairman, NASSCOM; co-founder, chairman and managing director, NIIT Group)

Twelve

Buoyed by our recent successes, I went back to Bombay and started hunting for a proper office to park ourselves in. It was during this time that we came across a modest 'For Rent' advert for a small 625-square-feet furnished office at Raheja Centre, a short distance from Nariman Point.

The location suited me and the boys, and I rushed to set up a meeting with the owner who had his office in the adjacent building.

Mr Chaganlal Sharma, the owner, turned out to be a man nearing his 70s and welcomed me warmly into his plush office. I put on my best behaviour—the typical educated and erudite Bengali emigrant to the city—and as we sat down over our customary cup of tea, I told the old man how a few of us, friends from IIT, had formed the company and how after a lot of struggle we had arrived at where we were.

The old man was taken in by my story and after praising me for my passion and zeal, wishing that his own sons had that, offered the place for a princely rent of ₹13,000 a month and an equally astounding rental deposit of ₹5 lakh.

I looked up sadly at Mr Chaganlal and told him that while we could somehow manage the rent, we simply didn't have that kind of money to put down on a rental deposit.

'Well, I like you, Mr Dasgupta,' he said, 'but I don't have time with me and anyway there are a bunch of people with ready cheques to take up that place, you know,' and with that called an end to our maiden meeting.

I walked away disappointed. The boys and I had really liked the office and there was no denying that it was situated in a plum location.

Scarcely had two days passed since our meeting when I heard Mr Chaganlal's weather-beaten voice waft over the telephone. 'You are a good man, Mr Dasgupta. I really liked you. Tell me what you can do and the office will be yours.'

'Well, as I had told you the other day, sir,' I replied into the mouthpiece, 'I will somehow manage the rent, but I can't afford the deposit that you are asking for. I can, at the very best put down ₹2 lakh and that too, after two months, but I would need to have the keys immediately.'

After a long silence at the other end, I heard his voice waft back, 'Are you kidding me, Mr Dasgupta? Who would be mad enough in Bombay to accept the kind of offer that you are making and that too, give up the keys before I have the monies in hand?'

The boys at the office who were privy to all this back and forth were getting increasingly desperate. They couldn't fathom why I was being so mulish and felt that the office space was slipping away from our grasp with every passing day. I chose to stick to my guns. There was a certain brinksmanship about me that I carry even today.

In about a week, Mr Chaganlal called again. 'Do something, Mr Dasgupta,' he pleaded. 'The office is waiting for you and the boys.'

'Mr Chaganlal, it has been kind of you to hold the place, but you know how hard-pressed we are,' I responded. 'I don't want you to suffer on my account, but can we do this? Let's peg the monthly rent at ₹15,000 instead of your request for 13. Meanwhile, I have been able to beg HO for one lakh rupees for the deposit, which I can give you this month and the next lakh will be at your door by the following month. That too, sir, would be after putting a huge strain on our finances.'

'Chalo, aap acche aadmi hain, deal nakki karte hai ispe (let's close the deal on this),' Mr Chaganlal replied, as the boys and I heaved a sigh of relief. We didn't waste any time and shifted into the office the very next day.

'Not a bad deal,' I thought as I congratulated myself. 'My learning is coming along fine and Mr Chaganlal has walked away a happy man though I did batter the old gentleman heavily on his asking price.'

Scarcely had a week had passed by when Mr Chaganlal chose to pay us a visit. He had a guy in tow lugging in a cabinet refrigerator, which he placed in my cabin. 'Only for you, Dasgupta sahib,' he said. 'The summer months can be cruel in Bombay.'

The kind-hearted gentleman passed away a few months after we had shifted over to the new office. He had left an indelible impression upon me with his compassion and thoughtfulness.

We stayed in that office for nine long years, even after we had grown to become one of the largest PC companies in India, the office transforming itself into a mascot for our western India team.

※

Thirteen

By 1987, we had built enough reserves from hawking electronic typewriters to finally start giving shape to our big dream—entering the computer hardware market—and giving the big boys a run for their money.

After all, we were computer people and selling typewriters didn't quite whet our appetite. Making money was never the singular point and never is to the serious ideas-driven entrepreneur.

Stephen and Mittal held the technology and delivery forts, while Anil fortified his national sales battalions. Dadan Bhai and I brought in the strategic marketing muscle with Dadan also dabbling in finance. Bharat Goenka took on the onus for all projects that came our way.

We started small with Stephen scouring the Taiwanese and Singapore markets for completely knocked down (CKD) and semi-knocked down (SKD) kits. Stephen did a marvellous job. In all his dealings, he made sure that we were always on the right side of the law and followed the draconian provisions of the then export-import (Exim) policy to the letter. India, in the 1980s, stretching well into its later years, was a closed economy and foreign exchange outgo was monitored through eagle eyes.

With Stephen around we were, most of the time, picture perfect in the pricing game and surely but steadily managed to break our dependence on the electronic typewriter business—a technology that was destined to be replaced by the much more versatile computer.

As our factory operations in Noida matured, we also started churning out server-grade machines. We made both MS-DOS and UNIX-based boxes and heartily competed with the big boys.

I believe it was Mittal who introduced us to Softek Ltd, one of India's first software companies to pioneer exclusively in software products. The founders again came from HCL's rich stables and in a short span of time they had managed to come up with an array of Indian version compilers for COBOL, FORTRAN, Pascal and Basic. Priced at a fraction of their western counterparts, we had their compilers pre-shipped with our UNIX and DOS boxes for demanding customers, saving us from setting up our own software R&D in the early years.

In time, Softek came up with a full suite of Office products (word processor, spreadsheet and database) for almost all UNIX variants of the day. This we bundled with our boxes, making them highly competitive.

◆

Singapore also turned out to be a happy hunting ground for us and we were helped a great deal by R. (Ambi) Srinivasan, who had just about set up Redington in those days. He proved to be a boundless friend and helped us in procuring both CKD and SKD kits, which we assembled back at our India factory and hawked the machines both in India and abroad.

As we grew in size and confidence, we started exploring the export market and made Singapore our temporary base camp. We were to later set up a fully-fledged operation there with our own office.

Our early export efforts focused on Russia, which turned out to be a lucrative market for us; both because of the bonhomie that India shared with the country and her distaste for anything American. Some of our largest offshore deals then came from Russia.

I remember two instances where our deal-making prowess made headlines. The first was a 2,000 PC deal from a Russian government agency (there weren't any private enterprises back then in Russia), followed up in quick succession with a 1,300 PC deal. I was fortunate enough to have spearheaded both those deals and it gave me rich insights into operating in international waters—something that was to come extremely handy a few years later.

In the midst of winning, there were also profound moments of defeat and dejection. It was Russia again that gave me one of my most agonising defeats.

Gazprom, which was set up in 1989 as a Russian government-owned company to exploit her rich natural gas reserves, had envisaged a keen interest in procuring around 2,000 powerful computers that came along with matrix graphic cards to perform complex operations. We were by then fairly entrenched in the Russian market and had emerged as one of the top contenders expected to bag the contract. It was a tough fight and we had to wrestle our way to the top.

I parked myself in Russia for a good part of six months chasing the order; delivering presentation upon presentation and attending innumerable meetings as we made our way through the Russian bureaucratic maze when I had my technical team fly in during the last two months of the final leg of the negotiations.

The team came armed with all sorts of sophisticated computer hardware equipment and we spent quite a packet on getting the desired graphics cards for demonstration. The guys did a great job and together we heaved our way to the very top where we found ourselves only in competition with one other firm that had made it to the summit.

With only the last hurdle to cross, the boys and I were supremely confident that we had snagged the deal. After all, we had slogged for over six months on this single case and had virtually met all of the client's requirements and more.

As I was ushered into the impressive boardroom at the Gazprom headquarters, I couldn't for a moment believe what I saw before me. Sitting on the opposite side, along with the board members of Gazprom, was a very familiar Indian gentleman, the founder director of the only other firm that had been left in the competition.

I knew from that point on that we were doomed and the meeting was just a formality that had to be dispensed with. I returned to the hotel almost in a daze. I still couldn't believe what I saw unfolding before me and broke down in tears. I sobbed unabashedly, berating God for doing this to us when we had fought our way to the top fairly and squarely.

Losing never affected me thus. I knew I could give as well as I got, but losing by trickery didn't quite suit my temperament. It had left a very bitter aftertaste.

Some two days later, I got a call from the Indian gentleman—the one who had wrecked our chances and had walked away with the prized trophy. He wanted to meet me at the International Hotel, the only other hotel, apart from where I had put up, that accepted dollar payments and was every bit a proper hotel that you could get in Russia those days.

Mr Ravinder Chamaria, the gentleman in question, was from Calcutta's enterprising Marwari community, and had built quite a reputation for himself as a trader for almost everything under the sun and had also bagged the distributorship for Epson's line of printers. He chose to operate from his offices in Singapore, from where he had spread his tentacles into Russian territory, selling all manner of electronic equipment that the Russians needed.

Uncanny and sharp, he had ingrained himself within the Russian bureaucracy and had thus been able to buy himself a board seat at Gazprom, catapulting himself from negotiating as a seller to a trusted negotiator for the buyer.

He greeted me warmly as we sat down for a chat and was effusive about my performance at Gazprom. He was contrite for his past actions as he raked up the subject saying, 'I did what I had to do...you had left me with no option and I felt the deal slipping away. With my future in Russia at stake, I had to play the last card that I had.'

'Let's forget it, Mr Chamaria,' I responded, lifting my glass to toast him. 'What matters is that you have the order and I do not. I have closed the books on this.'

'Not so easily, Mr Dasgupta. I have been very impressed with your performance and would like to make you an offer,' he said, as he sat nursing his glass.

He then proceeded to offer me half of his Singapore company, any salary that I thought would suit me and a fully paid for furnished house and a car of my choosing. All of it if I would come aboard and help manage and grow his company for him.

'That's a very kind offer that you make, Mr Chamaria, but I am very happy where I am,' I retorted. 'PCL happens to be my life and soul and I can't think of giving up on the dream that I have slogged for during the last few years.'

Mr Chamaria stared at me for a while, not believing his ears. He hadn't in his wildest dreams expected someone, at the prime of his life, to walk away from a deal such as this. He recovered from his thoughts with a smile and taking my hands said, 'I respect you for your sentiments, Mr Dasgupta, but should destiny offer up any opportunity for us to work together, I would just be a phone call away.'

As he walked me to the door, I shook his hands and told him, 'If I ever leave PCL and am on my own, you will be the first person that I shall call, and that's a promise.'

With that, I walked into the twilight-lit streets of Moscow, choosing to stroll to my hotel warmed at the thought that I hadn't lost as badly as I had berated myself for.

✍

Fourteen

With each passing year, we grew at a clipping rate, but there was still a distance to go before we caught up with the big boys. We were aggressive and hungry for growth and took our chances. The sales teams were given a free rein and they could offer pricing-based decisions on the spot. There was little or no bureaucracy involved. Each guy was privy to the pricing bandwidth and was trained to play the game.

Our standing instruction to the boys was, 'Feel free to walk into any of the directors' chambers if the competition is either HCL or Wipro. The rest should be dealt with by you. We have no time in our lives for the others. Period.' Such was our belief in ourselves. Some might call it arrogance.

We had our own way of bucking up the boys. During one of the oft-held review meets, I came across a sales guy who hadn't bagged a single order in the past quarter and the current month, too, promised to fare no better. I took the guy aside and told him, 'I know you have been working hard, but I find it hard to believe that it's just a run of bad luck that you are having. Why don't you have more faith in yourself? Why don't you believe it's possible for you to get more orders than those guys in the room? I know you can do it if you were only to tell yourself to go for it.'

The guy looked at me incredulously, expecting me to berate him, as I continued, 'Perhaps this target is too small and doesn't work for you,' and saying so, increased his quarterly target. The guy not only met his increased target but went on to become a top-ranking salesman at PCL.

◆

The Computer Society of India's 1990 silver jubilee exhibition gave PCL its first watershed moment. In many ways, we never looked back from then on.

Fresh out of our Goa conference where we had taken our entire staff, peon and all, for a three-day extravaganza, the guys did a fantastic job of catapulting PCL into the big league.

The Goa conference had a big impact on all of us and proved to be a huge morale booster. Our meetings would start at 11 a.m. and would end by 2 o' clock in the afternoon. After a lazy lunch and an afternoon of lolling around, doing pretty much nothing, we had the doors of the bar thrown open at 6 p.m. We partied till late in the night. We were a young company and proudly wore the badges of our success.

I have always believed that success begets success and there is nothing like celebrating your success with a certain abandonment that I find lacking today. I sometimes think we have been too sucked in by our digital world, abandoning the joys of human camaraderie.

CSI '90 gave me my first-opportunity to craft PCL's brand presence on a large-scale format. I had, during my travels abroad, felt awed by how our counterparts from the western world went about organising technological fairs and industrial exhibitions. Ours were staid in comparison and lacked in excitement and visitor interactions.

By the 1990s with the fast-expanding base of personal computers— PCs or desktops as they have come to be known—users needed a way to connect these machines and harness their combined power. Novell Netware running on MS-DOS provided a perfect environment. It allowed for both client-server architecture and peer-to-peer connectivity, which was a revolutionary move back then. Client-server architecture meant a single program or software could be accessed by all users on the network.

It also allowed users to share files and common resources such as printers among themselves, saving the hassle of running around with floppy disks to share files and content.

It was at CSI '90 that PCL launched the concept of distributed computing and client-server architecture. I modelled our presence based largely on how international companies showcased their prowess.

Used to the art of stage design from my IIT days, I designed for the first time an elevated platform some one-and-a-half feet off the ground to be accessed by a red-carpeted stair. To the right of the platform, we put up an impressive bank of 100 computers—all networked, and to the left created a cordoned off discussion area with an array of round glass tables with four to five sleek black chairs for each.

Our 2,000-square-feet display area at Taj Bengal stood head over its competition and for the first time again I used the nomenclature 'pavilion' instead of the oft-used term 'stall' to differentiate ourselves. PCL's pavilion was an instant hit and the huge glass bowl, sitting right in the middle of the pavilion, filled to the brim with toffees wrapped in PCL-lettered wrappers, proved to be one of the magnets that drew in the crowds.

Our discussion area transformed itself into a beehive of activity so much so that we had to restrict the crowds to pre-book their seats for the presentations that were held on the hour and every hour till the evening. We got flooded with enquiries and PCL became a name to reckon with its toffee wrappers strewn all across the hall.

I didn't quite stop at that and the team had to pull some serious strings to grant me my one non-negotiable wish. By the morning of the fair, we had put in place a gigantic gas-air balloon festooned at the top of Writers' Building, the government's seat of power in West Bengal, loudly proclaiming our brand and the power of distributed computing.

○∽○

I do recollect Bikram as being the least confrontational person, both within the Manufacturers Association of Information Technology (MAIT) and the industry. For the latter part, Bikram was probably the best foil to Dadan, who could be quite aggressive and they complemented each other very well. I am sure these qualities of being in competitive environments without getting into arguments and contentiousness must have stood him in great stead over the years.

Ashok Soota

(Former CEO, Wipro; former chairman, Mindtree; and currently founder and executive chairman, Happiest Minds)

Fifteen

WHILE THE GOING WAS GOOD and orders were pouring in, cash-flow management was giving us sleepless nights. Our bank balances were always next to nothing as we were accustomed to buying on credit, spending a significant amount of money on advertisements and staff costs and then selling in cash. Most of our operations were aided by the credit line thrown by bankers, but they too, had their limits.

It was like riding a tiger every day of our lives. Our lives depended on keeping our date with our aggressive sales targets, but all projections of targeted collections from customers would invariable go askew as clients stretched their payment dates, sometimes by weeks on end.

We were young and somewhat naïve. We knew what riding the tiger was, but no one had schooled us on how to get off the beast and so we carried on till one day Dadan called us for a board meeting.

Dadan was not the one for meetings and would always go around saying, 'Angrezi mein bara socho (Think big),' or in his characteristic Bhojpuri-laced Hindi say, 'Hoga ki nahi hoga, bas itna bolo (Just tell me if it is possible or not),' and it was thus a surprised lot that presented themselves for that, perhaps, our first structured board meeting.

Dadan was remarkably sombre and without much fussing about told us that we were tantalisingly close to tipping over the edge and that would be it. We had run up a debt of ₹32 crore and that both customer outstandings and pending supplier payments were at an all-time high. To cap it all, the bankers were now breathing down our necks.

A complete silence descended upon the room. Most of us didn't know what hit us, busy as we were chasing our dreams. Bharat was furious. Why, he questioned Dadan, had he kept the news under wraps for so long?

The room rapidly started filling up with smoke as we all lit our cigarettes, at a loss on what to do, when I said, trying to break the tension in the room, 'Closing down is an easy, no-brainer decision. Can't we think of something that is innovative and will pull us out of this mess?'

None of the ideas that were thrown around that day seemed to work until it was Dadan who came up with the gem: 'What we need is a big, and I mean a big multi-million dollar, order to heave us out of this hole. This would mean we export something.'

Easier said than done. India was a net importer and who had ever heard of Indians exporting electronics and hardware in such volumes to Americans? It all sounded so hair-brained that we all started smiling when I offered to take up the challenge. 'Let's give it a shot men and then we shall see...'

It was thus that I found myself on my first flight to the US to explore what fortunes the land of opportunity held for the beleaguered company.

My first pit stop was Harris County, Texas, home to the headquarters of Compaq. Founded by three senior managers from Texas Instruments, we had all agreed that it held the most promise for us. Compaq had held the distinction of being the youngest firm ever to make it to the Fortune 500 list in 1986, which was quickly followed up by hitting the $1 billion mark in revenue in 1987—the fastest company of that time to reach this milestone.

My initial meetings with Compaq went off well and I was introduced to a senior Indian executive to help take matters forward. We hit it off well as Compaq showed a keen interest in entering the Indian market and a willingness to compete with their arch-rivals, HP (Hewlett Packard), which had tied up with HCL to distribute their IBM-cloned PCs.

We hit our first snag when it came to Compaq procuring hardware from us. Their close partnership with Intel made it possible for them to ship PCs with the latest generation processor, keeping them ahead of the technology curve; procuring any sort of hardware from an Indian firm was something that wouldn't be kept on the table. Yes, we would get fabulous terms for distributing Compaq PCs—they had mastered the distribution game by staying away from direct retailing—but that meant nothing to us.

The most Compaq would do was to take either a CKD or SKD route and use our factories to help assemble their machines. 'No way could an Indian company step up to the plate and manufacture the quality of hardware that we are used to,' was their way of putting it, ending our tryst in disappointment for both of us.

My next call at Acer ended swifter than my meetings with the Compaq executives. The Taiwanese company baulked at my proposal and there I was on the streets again, clutching at my last hope—Dell Inc., the company that appeared at the end of my list.

As much as I was disappointed with the outcome of my efforts at Compaq and Acer, I had learnt a vital lesson. In most (if not all) computer manufacturing companies, the marketing and production/engineering arms operated as if they inhabited singularly isolated islands, only coming once in a while to the mainland to meet the top chiefs. For the rest, they were individual units operating at their own whims and fancies.

If I was to succeed in Dell, I had to meet their chief Michael Dell. Meeting with the heads of either marketing or engineering would end in futility. I needed someone who could see and appreciate the big picture and help bring both the marketing and engineering units on the same page.

The roadmap was clear. I either manage to meet Michael Dell or come back empty-handed. A very binary decision, I told myself on my flight to Austin, Texas, the headquarters of Dell Inc. This time around I took Ranjana along, something that I didn't do very often during my business trips abroad.

By the time we reached Texas, I had scoured through the entire Exim policy of the government and had found an obscure clause buried within the mountain of ink that promised to hold some light.

Meeting Michael, up at his ninth-floor castle, would be an uphill task but I had to find a way to meet him and I racked my brains to figure out a way to do so. The easiest would be through someone he trusted and I could think of no one except Richardson, the vice president of international sales—the only one who had shown some interest in meeting an unknown Indian.

Richardson turned out to be a very warm and effusive person and we quickly got to know each other well. I knew that pushing him too much to give me business would only end up in disappointment and I stuck to my agenda of having Richardson take me to his CEO.

'Meeting Michael would be very difficult, Bikram, but I can, for friendship's sake, take you to the lady who manages his office and from then on you are very much on your own, pal,' he said rising from his chair.

'Suits me,' I told him as we made our way to the elevator bank.

෴

Sixteen

MICHAEL'S SECRETARY TURNED OUT to be a pretty young lady with a charming smile. 'He is Bikram,' Richardson said, introducing me. 'He is from India and is a friend. We are talking business with him…I will leave the rest of the talking to Bikram,' he said as he took leave of us.

'You are such a sweetheart for meeting me,' I told the beaming lady as I launched into my pitch—a pitch that somehow came gushing forth. 'I have a one-point agenda here. I am an entrepreneur from India and I would really like to meet Michael, one who has not only a built a $800 million company that is only growing but also the person who could afford to buy himself a BMW at the age of 17 for cash.' At this, the lady burst out laughing and I knew that I had made my inroads with her.

'Surely you wouldn't grudge a man who has travelled 10,000 miles a 10-minute meeting,' I said, throwing her my warmest smile.

She took a hard look at me before saying, 'Okay, here's the deal. Michael has a meeting with the stockbrokers from 10 to 11 and usually has his lunch at 12. I have kept some slack in his day's schedule since his newborn kid isn't keeping well and he needs to check back every once in a while with his wife. I will slot you in during the break. Just walk in and the rest is up to you.'

'Thank you! You are a real sweetheart,' I said as I took a seat in the waiting area, not believing my luck as I checked off the first point in my agenda.

It was around a little over 11.15 a.m. when Dell's secretary signalled me to walk into his capacious office.

It was the longest walk in my life as I strode into his office. 'Shoot,' said the twenty-six-year-old multimillionaire as soon as we had shaken hands.

Extremely affable and approachable, Michael Dell was easy to talk to and he listened with keen interest to what I had to say. As the minutes rolled by, we found ourselves swapping stories of our own entrepreneurial journeys and my 10-minute slot with Michael stretched out into two full hours.

Lunch was a distant thought as we discussed Dell's entry into India. With HP, Dell's foremost competitor tying up with HCL, and IBM already on Indian shores, it was important that Dell make an impact in one of the world's most promising markets. But a combination of red tape, steep import tariffs and a viable distribution network had kept him away.

If Dell were to make serious inroads into India, it had to compete on price and quality.

Dell being Dell, quality was a no-brainer, given their rigid testing and evolved customer support systems, but pricing was a huge roadblock. Since Dell wasn't your classical nuts and bolts manufacturer and relied heavily on importing a significant number of parts from Taiwan, its prices in India would, by definition, be at par with its western counterparts, if not higher. This did not quite suit Dell's strategy and thus they had held back from aggressively addressing the then nascent Indian market.

It was at this juncture that I fished out the golden nugget of information that I had gleaned from my laborious study of the Exim policy manual. The then policy allowed for a 50 per cent tariff reduction on every $25 of imports for every $100 of exports. Simply stated, if a firm exported $10 worth of goods, they could import $2.5 worth of goods at 50 per cent of the prevailing import duty rates.

My proposition was simple on the face of it. 'We will,' I told Michael Dell, 'use the import tariff subsidy to import Dell machines and export full populated motherboards to Dell.'

'That would not only give Dell a significant pricing advantage vis-à-vis the competition but also allow you to capture a significant section of the black market that operated due to the pricing advantage.'

In the preceding days, I had spent agonising hours with Stephen on the phone, debating what should be our 'manufacturing' proposition to Dell. SMPS (switch mode power supply) boxes were too basic and floppy drives were too complicated. We finally hit upon manufacturing motherboards—it had 150–160 parts, needed some degree of expertise and automation and frankly happened to be the lowest hanging fruit.

'This,' I told an interested Michael Dell, 'would be the only way in which you can enter the Indian market and capture a share of it.'

Not one to dilly-dally on something that caught his imagination, Michael called for his vice-president-production, and the executive vice-president-international sales, Mr Andrew Harris. I mentally checked off the second item on the agenda.

'This is what Bikram has to say,' said Michael, explaining my proposition to them. 'Does this make sense, guys?'

'We anyways import motherboards,' chipped in the vice-president production. 'If these guys can do it at a lower cost and at a better quality, we are okay.'

'We can assure you of better quality and lower dead on arrivals (DoAs), but we can't possibly do it at a lower cost,' I said, turning my attention to the head of production. 'We manufacture a measly 15 motherboards a month and the guys that you buy from produces 10,000 of them a month. We simply can't match them on the component price.'

'But,' I said, taking a heavy pregnant pause, 'if you were to make us Dell's approved vendor and pass along your approved list of component suppliers with the instruction that they supply to us at the same price as they do to the guy that manufactures your motherboards in Taipei, only then can we hope to succeed.'

'And,' I continued, not wanting to break the momentum that I had gained, 'we shall do more. We will have an open BOM policy only for Dell.'

'What is an open BOM, Bikram?' asked the intrigued production head. Till that moment, even I didn't know what an open BOM was. The words had mystically popped into my head and out it came into the vast open universe. BOM for the uninitiated denotes the 'bill of material' or more simply, a list of parts, their quantities and costs that go in to manufacturing any product.

'Well, this is how it works,' I said, sounding every bit the erudite technologist. 'We shall share with you the detailed BOM for every kind of motherboard that we manufacture for Dell and I will load a 15 per cent margin on it. That's the deal.'

'No one, I can assure you, will open their BOMs to you and you can't be sure if they make a margin of 15 or 30 per cent. I ask for 15 per cent since that is the bare minimum that we need to survive,' as I added tongue-in-cheek, 'if you were to give me more, we would be more than willing...'

The production head nodded in agreement and said, 'Sure, if we give you business, we better make sure that you guys survive.'

Michael, who had been listening to this animated discussion, suddenly rose from his desk and said, 'Stop. Stop. Take this discussion to your table, guys,' adding, 'but Bikram, I want to do business with you' and saying so, raised his thumb to his two executives as we stepped out.

What followed were three days of hectic negotiations, interacting upwards of 12 hours each day, as we worked on each nut and bolt of the deal. I was at the peak of my energy, focus and concentration. I truly believed that it was not only a watershed moment for us at PCL, but a game-changing moment for India as a whole.

I had never worked at those levels of energy and concentration before and have not since. As I reflect back, I see in this a moment of divinity, as if a higher power was directing and controlling my moves and actions— all seemingly orchestrated to achieve a singular goal.

Meticulous to the last detail, I had to face an 11-member Dell team as we negotiated every cost detail. I would often get into lengthy calls with Stephen to help make sense of the numbers. He was of great help.

Stephen being a man of detail—both in explanation and work—I often found myself pleading with him to spare me the lengthy explanations and tell me 'the price at which we will not lose money' and 'what I should be staying off from.'

By the morning of the third day, the finer contours of the deal had started emerging and we were looking at a $20 million contract. But I wanted more. Having come thus far, I was unwilling to let go of the rope that destiny had handed me without trying to increase both the size and duration of the contract. This was vitally important if we were to jump into bed with some of the biggest bankers to fund our ambitious dreams.

Turning my attention to David Beasley, the gentleman Dell had tasked with ensuring that the deal happened, I told him, 'Here is the story, David. It will take six months or thereabouts to build our new factory and get the machinery in. This would call for substantive investments, which I believe should pay itself back in the next five to six years. So, this is how it stacks up...We have a pre-operative period of six months before we can get production started, then the twelve-month deal that we have on the table kicks off. But it would make sense to all of us, the bankers included, if we can have a two-year contract, which would in essence mean a 30-month contract taking in the pre-operative period.'

'Makes an awful lot of sense,' said David, 'we have to buy anyway' and smiling, continued, 'DoAs are DoAs and your headache pal.'

What remained to be sealed was the numbers and I was reminded of what Dadan Bhai had done so neatly in the Guwahati computer deal and decided to adopt the same technique.

As we assembled back after a break, I told David and Richardson, who had peeked in to see how we were chugging along, 'As far as numbers go, we already have agreed on $20 million for the first year and given that we shall only grow, can we agree on a $30 million for the next 12 months?'

'Sure,' said Richardson, 'I don't see why not.'

Thus was born in November 1991 India's first truly 'Make in India' hardware export deal. At $50 million, it was the largest hardware export contract of its day—a deal that had a deal within a deal, with PCL being appointed Dell's authorised nationwide distributor for its computers in India. It was an all-round win-win proposition for both the partners.

For PCL, it meant a colossal export deal, a contract that catapulted our brand equity sky high, giving us access to the latest production technologies and a highly prized distributorship from one of the world's fastest growing PC companies.

For Dell, it meant hedging its supply risk by having an additional manufacturing base away from Taiwan; additionally, we were the only supplier to perpetually give back 25 per cent of the business received. It also meant very little investments for Dell as they made headway into the vast but highly competitive Indian PC market.

By 4.30 p.m., we had arrived at the final contract and the photographers were called in. As we toasted this new relationship, it was Andrew Harris who made the most telling remark. He raised a toast to me saying, 'We hadn't yet met a guy from India who came with an empty bag and walked out with a $50 million deal. We have never in our lives witnessed an incident like this.'

I raised a toast to him saying, 'You say you haven't seen an incident like this. I, for one, hadn't dreamt of this!'

I returned to the hotel that evening, exhausted and drained of any energy. Ranjana met me at the door. She knew about the stakes involved and had waited with bated breath to know the final outcome. I flung the mint-new contract on the bed as I slumped into a chair. 'I have done it!' was all that I could say, to her delight and relief.

That evening, I took Ranjana out for dinner to a quaint Italian restaurant, famous for serving homemade wine, which we had been eyeing. I had promised to bring her here if we cracked the deal. The restaurant proved every bit of its name, its wine excellently paired with a range of authentic Italian dishes.

We didn't talk much as we savoured the wine and the food. I felt a strange calm enveloping me. I was finally at peace with myself.

It was a historic day for me, PCL and the Indian IT industry. In some ways, I felt a new India was born with 'We can export hardware' written all over it.

As the night progressed, the magnitude of what I had single-handedly managed to achieve started sinking in. The single $50 million contract was by far the largest hardware export contract that any entrepreneurial firm in India could manage to win.

∽

If there is one person that exuded confidence, joy and hope while carrying the huge burden of the Indian IT hardware industry during its formative years, it has to be my friend, Bikram Dasgupta. When you were down in spirits, lost for next step, and submerged in your sorrow and misfortune, you just had to pick up your phone and connect with Bikram. You would emerge from that conversation smiling, confident about the future, and ready to conquer the world. Bikram and his wonderful family are lighting up Kolkata's IT scene with their dedication to IT professionals and their charity. I wish the old, the middle-aged and the young members of the Bikram Dasgupta's family the best of everything.

N.R. Narayana Murthy
(Padma Vibhushan and Padma Shri Awardee.
Founder and ex-Chairman, Infosys)

Seventeen

It was on a cold but sunny December Delhi morning that Dadan Bhai met me at the airport. He hugged me tightly saying, 'I want to kiss you…I don't know what to do with you now!'

Some 14 months later, I found myself back at the ninth-floor office of Michael Dell, in Austin, Texas. This time, I had taken along the first motherboard from our new plant.

'Does this work?' he asked.

'Sure does,' I replied, smiling.

The motherboard had gone through Dell's rigorous quality assurance processes and had been subjected to a battery of tests using Dell's automated testing equipment.

'Give it back to the store on your way down, Bikram, it cost me $160,' he said, smiling as he stood shaking my hands, his eyes moistening up, as was mine.

Our deal with Dell made banner headlines and I suddenly found myself being feted as the new poster boy of the Indian IT industry.

There was not a single morning that I didn't see myself smiling from a newspaper or magazine article. Such was the euphoria over the deal. Even our arch-rivals grudgingly agreed that we had come up with a plum. It shook up the industry from its deeply entrenched belief that Indian companies were incapable of manufacturing electronics that stood up to the quality demands of the western world.

I enjoyed every bit of being in the limelight. I loved the glare of the television studios and the clamouring of the press folk for a sound bite. I made no pretensions of being modest and oozed confidence with a whole lot of bravado thrown in as I breezed my way in my interactions with the media and the public.

Always a good orator, I found myself being invited to conferences and seminars as a keynote speaker, with people vying for my attention.

I was suddenly the face of PCL, smiling down from billboards, newspapers and trade magazines. PCL had become synonymous with my name and my work moniker 'BDG' became my de facto name. It all came to such a pass that even people from the press started to know me by my moniker.

It was a week since I had come from the US after striking the deal that I got a call from the Prime Minister's Office or the PMO as it is popularly known. The prime minister had wished to meet me over a cup of tea, the caller informed me over the telephone.

'Man, have you arrived!' I told myself. The prime minister—the most powerful being who sat over the fates of nearly a billion people then—wanted to have tea with me? I had come a long way from a being unknown Bengali from a small industrial town of Bengal to a 30-year-old entrepreneur being hosted to tea by the PM.

I arrived much before time to the PM's office at 7, Race Course Road and had to navigate through the huge maze of security that protected the man. I was amazed at the level of security at each checkpoint as they went through me with a fine-tooth comb.

As I sat with Mr P.V. Narasimha Rao, the ninth prime minister of India, we discussed the impending liberalisation of the Indian economy and his vision of India's place in the global community. A scholarly man with a soft demeanour, he could speak an astounding 17 languages and was widely acknowledged as the harbinger of economic reforms in India along with Dr Manmohan Singh, another brilliant economist and an erstwhile Reserve Bank of India governor, who later went on to become India's 13th PM, who Rao had installed as his finance minister to usher in a slew of structural reforms for the economy.

Buoyed by the success of the Dell deal, I had overlooked how resilient India's red tape could be and hit the first of many hurdles when I put in our application to set up a 100 per cent export-oriented unit (EOU).

The EOU operations would help us export our motherboards to Dell and in turn make PCL eligible for 50 per cent rebate on the prevailing import duty tariff, on 25 per cent of imports vis-à-vis the total export value.

This I had promised to Michael Dell to plough back to import and market in India fully kitted Dell machines at prices that would beat our rivals hollow.

The bureaucracy, in its wisdom, decided that PCL wouldn't be eligible for any such import duty tariff rebates since we were exporting motherboards and re-importing fully kitted computers, two entirely different kinds of goods in their view.

Fortuitously, during this time, I came in touch with Mr Rahul Khullar, an extremely bright 1975 batch Indian Administrative Service officer whom Dr Manmohan Singh, the then finance minister, had appointed as his secretary, to help carry out the first round of economic reforms.

I had found a kindred and an erudite soul in Mr Khullar, and over many meetings with him and his team, I explained how motherboards were an integral part of computers and it just didn't make sense to see its various parts as separate and distinct units.

It would be, I told them, akin to owning a car without an engine or wheels or for that matter any of the multitude of parts that made a car a car.

Thus prodded, the mandarins at South Block decided to revisit their old rule book and used a term of my coinage—'broad banding'— to bring such items under a single umbrella category. This proved to be a huge relief to the fast-growing PC industry in India and opened the nation's door to enterprising young entrepreneurs who could now choose to manufacture and export individual components that made up the modern computer.

In some ways, this also became a precursor to the long meetings that I held with Mr Khullar and other top-ranking bureaucrats to help give shape to India's nascent IT policy and get rid of the red tape that surrounded import of electronic goods and components.

Back at PCL, the newness of what we had achieved had us all fired up. Come thus far, I was not willing to give up on the Dell opportunity and I immersed myself in the task of setting up our new EOU factory in the Mahipalpur Industrial Area near the Delhi–Gurgaon border.

Ramping up production from a measly 15 motherboards a month to nearly 10,000 was a mammoth task in 1992 and we went in for a great deal of automation. It was for the first time that we moved to surface mount technology (SMT), a much faster and automated method of producing electronic circuits. SMT allowed components to be mounted or placed directly onto the surface of printed circuit boards instead of the archaic through-hole technology method of fitting components with wire leads into holes in the circuit board.

As the factory took shape and we got close to starting production, I assembled all the Altos engineers and their wives for a tour of the new factory and addressing them, said, 'I would request you, for the sake of your husbands' career growth besides the obvious growth of the organisation, that you allow for a great deal of disruption in your family lives in the coming 11 months, since we would be spending more time here, under the roof of this factory than at our homes to meet our commitment to Dell. I will return to you your husbands every weekend, but with the promise that I get them back in shape on Monday morning.'

They all smiled. None of the members assembled that day spoke in a contrarian voice and I felt blessed in many ways. This is what a transformation contract can do, I reminded myself.

◆

If I was thrust into the limelight, it was to Dadan Bhai's credit that he didn't grudge me taking the torch away from him. 'You are better at this, Dasgupta Seth,' he would say. 'Given to me, I would surely screw it up.'

My newfound fame gave me lifelong friends, but it also attracted its fair share of detractors. Not everyone took kindly to the kind of aggression and naked ambition that I displayed. I did not fake modesty and if I was hard on myself, I was equally hard on others. I found mediocrity stifling.

I use mediocrity not in the sense of the term that it is often used, but to denote one's refusal to budge from straight-line thinking or their apparent immunity to any measure of motivation to go beyond their limitations.

My firebrand image had its drawbacks too, as I found myself appointed as the chairman of the exhibitions committee of the Manufacturers Association of Information Technology (MAIT), the IT industry's premier industry body back then.

It happened to be the dowdiest of all the committees and a place where I could, or so the thinking went, cause the least trouble given my penchant to always push the system to think beyond regular geometric shapes.

Eighteen

WHILE THE IT INDUSTRY IN INDIA was still in its infancy, it did not deter brave hearts from jumping into the trudging bandwagon, and the early 1990s witnessed a spurt in the number of new companies being incorporated. The industry then revolved very much around the hardware business and was very domestic in its customer base.

This gave rise to a piquant situation. Operating as we were in a small, price-sensitive market, the Indian customer—always a sharp and streetwise fellow—started playing off the competition against each other. We spilled a lot of blood on the streets as sales executives limped away with slender thin margins. Some deals went into a furious spin and called for protracted negotiations, while some went hurtling down south.

The customers knew that they had an upper hand and preyed on our vulnerabilities. They delayed payments and delayed ordering, and with talent in short supply, competitors rampantly poached employees off each other. There was little that the industry captains could do except rue their luck and moan endlessly during the executive council meetings of MAIT.

It was during one such meeting, in July 1993, that it struck Pradeep Kar, Microland's founder, Pravin Gandhi of Digital India and me that an attempt to informally bring together the CEOs of the IT industry, over healthy dosages of beer, might just prove to be a better solution to address our industry woes and common challenges instead of being stuck within the confines of a structured industry body organisation like MAIT.

Beer was to be the lubricant of choice to help create an almost frictionless bond of personal friendship that would pave the way to bilaterally address prickly issues of competition, poaching, cross outstandings, et al.

Our call to arms was answered by 11 CEOs who happened to be in Bangalore (now Bengaluru) and we met at 6 p.m. at Pub World, a hip and cool hangout on Residency Road, Bangalore.

By the time the 11 of us were ready to stagger out of the pub, we had given birth to a very bubbly BAIT (a neat parody of MAIT) or the Beer Drinkers Association of Information Technology.

Our clarion call had attracted the best minds in the business and the first BAIT meeting held in July 1993 had Pravin Gandhi, Pradip Kar, Vijay Thadani, Nandan Nilekani, Sridhar A.V., Kapil Jain, Anal Jain, Anurag Agarwal, Dinesh Puri, Vikas Deshmukh and Bhaskar Pramanik.

BAIT was fun and informal and we all agreed that crystal ball gazing would be among the foremost activities of the group. Meeting minutes were duly noted down on the pub's paper napkins and we came up with quaint rules and terms.

DOS or the disk operating system transformed itself into 'drown our sorrows' or at times 'double our sorrows'. IBM's inspiration tagline 'Think' transmuted itself into 'Drink' and to everyone's delight, the paper work heavy ISO 9000 became In Search (of) Outstanding (anything greater than ₹9,000).

The rules were simple and elegant. A meeting, to be considered legal, would need a quorum of two members. The hoi polloi were to be kept at bay by keeping membership restricted to invitation only or to those with a minimum of 10 years of IT experience. Females were welcome, but would be strictly referred to as Ms and not Mrs.

The minor rules enshrined upon each member to drink no fewer than six glasses of draught beer. No other kind of beer or for that matter any variety of hard drinks would do. Meetings needed to be kicked off latest by 7.30 in the evening and disbanded no later than 10 p.m. Dinner was what your wives/husbands cooked!

We had even managed to coherently articulate our vision statement for BAIT. It stood thus:

'Little blurred but will clear. When we don't know. But we have hope.'

All this bonhomie and camaraderie had its serious side as well.

BAIT did more to lay a strong foundation for the Indian IT industry than people may know or care to remember. It built an enduring companionship within the ranks of India's leading IT thinkers and brought them together to solve problems in a friendly environment. BAIT ensured that we remained firmly customer-focused, but not at the cost of each other.

A salute to Bikram from a fellow BAITer...Lots of sweet memories of working together... managing the complex relationship between MAIT, NASSCOM and *Business India* in the IT Asia days... rallying the industry buddies together at BAIT....being ever ready to help a friend in need.

Bikram loves to live on the edge and thrives on solving seemingly impossible problems. He is an aggressive salesman, yet his customers love him; he is a strong negotiator, yet closes with a touch of magnanimity.

Indeed a 'Limited Edition', he builds lasting relationships stamped with his inimitable blend of genuine concern, affection and trust.

Vijay K. Thadani
(Director and co-founder, NIIT Technologies)

Nineteen

STRADDLED WITH THE DOWDY EXHIBITIONS committee at MAIT, I decided it was time someone did something about the way IT exhibitions were held in the country. CSI '90 at Taj Bengal, Calcutta, had given me a first-hand account of the power of a well-organised trade show and I, as the chairman of IT Asia, was determined to make a difference to how MAIT organised its exhibitions.

I truly believed that the gradual coming of age of the Indian IT industry, free from the fetters of governmental regulations and buoyed by the sheer positivity of private enterprise, should be branded and marketed if we were to position ourselves favourably in the world. We could no longer afford to be seen as the slumbering Indian elephant.

In this Taiwan, Germany and the USA had one thing in common. They all had their marquee IT trade shows that were thronged by millions of visitors and millions of dollars of business transacted. These trade shows gave the user community a first-hand experience of what the technologists were up to and they could interact with the most valued and innovative companies and products.

Sadly, nothing of that calibre existed in India and companies managed to make do with the culture of roadshows that was first introduced by Amit Dutta Gupta of HCL.

This called for a healthy bout of unconventional thinking and turning things on their heads. 'Not a very auspicious brief to give to men too used to the familiarity of doing things along predictable lines,' I remember saying to myself as I called for a meeting of the exhibition committee to plan for the annual IT exhibition that was held by MAIT.

Change is always difficult to bring about, but I always had a dogged persistence and a belief that a handful of men were enough to turn the tide of things. Yes, you needed to have a certain degree of purity in your thinking and the ability to think beyond your immediate personal or company gains if you wanted to do something that was truly transformational and had an impact on society and community at large.

I was fortunate enough to be in the midst of a few like-minded peers who were as enthusiastic as I was and we set about the task of transforming the face of technology exhibitions in India.

It was perhaps for the first time that our motley band dared to think big—really big—and we moved the exhibition to the large fair grounds of Pragati Maidan in New Delhi. Inaugurated in 1972 by the then Prime Minister Indira Gandhi, and spread over 150 acres with more than 6,25,000 square feet of exhibition space, it was an ideal venue to showcase India's growing prowess in information technology.

We also gave the exhibition a new name—one that was to resonate with the increasing clout of the Indian IT industry in the years to follow. We named the fair IT Asia and in naming it so, took a pole position among Asian nations to showcase our nation's IT talent.

IT Asia '92 heralded an entirely new era of IT exhibitions in India. Spread over multiple pavilions, visitors—both businessmen and common folk—had an opportunity to see a galaxy of international and Indian brands showcase their wares—from hardware to software, each piece of the IT chain was on display.

Emboldened by our success in IT Asia '92, we planned an even bigger event for IT Asia '93. This time around, we had the then Prime Minister P.V. Narasimha Rao inaugurate what turned out to be India's marquee technology exhibition. That year, we had a footfall of about 143,000 business visitors and up to 143 Indian and international companies showcasing their products.

It was in the midst of IT Asia '94 that I received a lunch invite from Shiv Nadar. As we sat in his plush office having lunch, Shiv said, 'Bikram, you have done what you do best. You have established another superb milestone by setting up "exhibitions" as yet another platform and a new benchmark for the Indian IT Industry. You should now move to newer things as there are many who can take things forward, now that you have them shown the way. Well done!'

Shiv's words that afternoon would prove to be prophetic.

IT Asia '94 would go on to become an even more momentous event for us and a hugely significant watershed moment in my life. I had throughout my chairmanship of IT Asia from 1992 to 1994 proved that we could only be limited by our thinking.

Yes, fate and luck have their fair share in the game of life, but then 'determination' coupled with strong 'self-belief' have a way of tugging at destiny's heartstrings.

✑

Twenty

It WOULD BE WHOLLY UNTRUE if I don't admit that I didn't get carried away by the attention that I found myself surrounded with. I enjoyed every bit of being in the spotlight and thrived off its energy. It felt good to be known and recognised.

In the process of being recognised and feted by the community, the media and to some degree my own expressions, were instrumental in creating a 'larger-than-life' persona—something that I came dangerously close to identifying myself with had it not been for my family, especially Ranjana.

In my quest to heave myself up from my ordinary middle-class upbringing, there was also some deep-rooted subliminal proving to be done. My scholarly and egalitarian-minded father had always eschewed all signs of ostentation and bitterly derided those who chose to do so.

My brother and I (and later our wives) had grown to hear Baba often repeat the Bengali phrase '*Bitto holae chitto haray*'. Roughly translated, it meant 'losing one's soul (in the pursuit of) to wealth'.

I always believed that it was stretching a point too far and that both wealth and the purity of soul could be maintained and had to be proved to be doing so. This proved to be a vexing conundrum later in my life and I have always struggled to balance business practicality with the dictates of answering to one's soul.

Ranjana was much simpler and in your face. In the midst of all my trapezeing in the air, she simply said, 'I don't know who BDG is. I have been married to Bikram and it is with Bikram that I shall be very happy to relate myself with,' sending me crashing down to earth.

How do you thank someone who could make such a simple statement, yet have such a profound impact?

Back at PCL, life was moving at a hectic pace and our newfound confidence (and access to money) made Dadan decide to take the next big plunge—listing PCL on the Bombay Stock Exchange. The IPO turned out to be a huge success and was oversubscribed to many times over. The company was flush with money and contracts.

Our deal with Dell had catapulted us to an entirely new high and we had tie-ups in place with Microsoft, Novell, Motorola and 3 Com, thus uniquely positioning us to offer single-window hardware and software solutions to our corporate clients. Institutional sales became our strongest forte and we were well on our way to be crowned the No. 1 PC company in India.

But then, things started to change. I noticed a change in Dadan Bhai's interactions with me. No longer was he as effusive and we would often part ways from a meeting with disagreements. This had never happened before since it was an easy relationship that we had shared.

Dadan started resenting my larger-than-life persona and the halo that surrounded my moniker 'BDG'. PCL was, after all, something that he had germinated.

Was Dadan wrong in his thinking? Perhaps not. What would I have done had I been in his place? Maybe exhibit the same, if not more of the same behaviour.

I insisted that PCL settle down and adopt processes and systems that make organisations mature and stable. We couldn't afford to 'shoot and scoot' any longer. I had seen how serious Dell was about its processes and the premium that it placed on quality and customer service. Dadan disagreed. For him, it was the 'rezult', in his characteristic Bhojpuri-laden Hindi, that mattered. Processes came later, if at all. You lived only to sell.

These small disagreements gave way to larger differences. We knew software was the road to walk, but we vastly differed in our approaches. I resented the reckless funding mindset that Dadan had for the software business. Why should you put your existing businesses at risk by recklessly pouring money into a new business—a business that didn't yet have a coherent business plan?

By early 1994, Baba's often-used maxim about 'wealth and the soul' started to kick in. We had raised an awful lot of money, but we weren't kept fully in the loop on its deployment. Money had suddenly changed Dadan's way of viewing things.

It was a strange and wholly different Dadan that I choose not to remember.

Anil Bhushan Chopra, our co-founder and sales champion, had perhaps chosen the best route. He quit soon after the IPO, taking his share along with him. 'I have had enough of running around the Ferris wheel,' he would say. 'I will now play golf for the rest of my life.'

Things rapidly started going south between Dadan and me. Bharat Goenka, too, was getting restive. The lack of financial transparency and Dadan's sometimes reckless way with funds did not bode well for the company. I didn't quite like the smell of it.

Not one to burden my family with the vicissitudes of a workplace, I found it difficult to keep things to myself and gradually confided in Ranjana. She carried a sensible head on her shoulders and was not easily swayed by emotion.

Despite all the commotion between Dadan and me, we didn't let business suffer. I must say it was to Dadan's credit that he did not bring out our differences in public and I maintained my external demeanour with him. By the end of 1994, we had managed to make PCL the No. 1 PC company in India.

It was also during this time that I tried to help the company make sense of its new business line. It irked Dadan and he didn't take kindly to my trying to be helpful. He perhaps felt that letting me into the new venture would only result in me taking the limelight away from him. He had been witness to my single-handedly swinging the Dell deal and the media frenzy that followed.

He thus started putting vexing irritants in my way that over time took on serious proportions.

✑

Twenty-one

I WOKE UP TO A BRIGHT DELHI morning eagerly looking forward to what was to be an exciting day ahead of me. IT Asia '94 was proving to be an even bigger success than IT Asia '93. This time around, as the chairman of IT Asia for the third consecutive year, my team and I had managed to invite Mr Pranab Mukherjee, the industries minister (later to be elected as the 13th president of India), to inaugurate the fair. It bode well for the industry captains as they eagerly took this opportunity to share their industry concerns with him in a rare one-on-one basis.

The evening promised to be even better. I had set up a meeting with a team of senior executives from a major international powerhouse; a company that I had been cultivating for the past few months. Should the deal come through, our fledgling software dreams would get a huge leg-up.

Inviting the team over to IT Asia '94 seemed to me a natural way to give them a first-hand impression of India's growing IT prowess as much as it was to show off mine, and in turn PCL's, organisation skills and the political clout that we could wield.

I had made careful plans for the evening. My guests had indicated their predilection for north Indian food and I had booked our seats at one of Delhi's most glitzy restaurants, famous for serving the best and most authentic north Indian cuisine in India.

I desired to give my guests an experience that they would remember. Americans, I had realised over my innumerable trips to the US, loved the informality of closing deals over a glass of wine and good food.

The evening commenced just as I had arranged. I had forewarned the maître d'hôtel about my meeting and he ensured that my guests were given the treatment of modern-day maharajas.

It delighted my guests to be treated thus and we soon found ourselves animatedly discussing doing business in India. My guests were excited at the prospect of tapping the emergent software talent pool and I could sense a deal in the making.

All of a sudden, a somewhat inebriated Dadan Bhai made his appearance and slumped into the chair that I had kept reserved for him. It was not the usual chirpy Dadan Bhai that I knew. He appeared grumpy and chose to speak in monosyllables, seemingly uninterested in the proceedings.

My guests were taken aback. They had not expected this dreary welcome, least of all from the CEO of the No. 1 PC company in India. It must have seemed that Dadan had been nagged into the meeting, one that he held of little value.

The gaiety that surrounded the table just moments back was suddenly enveloped in an embarrassed silence. None of us spoke. There was nothing to speak about.

Dadan had known that I was closing in on the scent of an impending deal and he, the sharp fellow that we was, had me wondering if all of this was a pre-planned act to throw a spanner in the works.

Mercifully my guests, realising my predicament, spared me the embarrassment of tarrying any longer. We bid our goodbyes to Dadan and as I saw them off to their car I thought, 'There you go, Bikram, you wanted to give them a memorable evening and what a memorable one it was!'

I couldn't get myself to return to the restaurant to confront Dadan. The damage had been done.

I shooed away my driver, preferring to walk my way home. I couldn't in my wildest imagination believe that Dadan could do this to me and by extension to PCL. PCL was a dream that we had lovingly nurtured brick by brick and to see it being gnawed at its roots was too much to take.

I couldn't fathom Dadan's motive behind his act. PCL had been his brainchild—one that he had led from the front as the senior-most and unquestionable leader, but why this? Was something bothering him deeply or had I failed him in some way? Why?

As I walked into the night, the gods refused to yield any answers to my fervent stream of questions. My eyes welled up with tears, and I cried unabashedly, asking myself why? Why? Why?

Suddenly, out of nowhere, the sky opened itself up to a torrential shower. The darkness of the skies reflecting the darkness that I felt within me. PCL was my life, the only life that I knew.

I was thoroughly drenched by the time I knocked on my doorbell. I must have looked every bit a madman as Ranjana shrank back on seeing me.

'What happened?' she asked anxiously.

◆

That night, as I and Ranjana sat discussing the disaster and what it meant for me and the family, Rahul, the elder of the twins, sheepishly walked into the room and said, in his child-like innocence, 'Dad, why don't you give up that which is hurting you so much?'

I patted my child on his head and had him head to his room to join his brother. A child had made simple of a burden that I was carrying so long.

Sleep was difficult to come by that night and as I lay awake staring at the ceiling, occasionally lightened by the headlights of a passing automobile, my heart refused to yield to the inevitability that I saw before me.

I had always believed that the pantheon of Gods above had helped steer my boat, sheltering me in their cove during the harshest of storms and I, on my part, had kept my mind and heart from veering off in different directions, dedicating myself to the purity and divinity that I found in work. I saw no reason to blame Him for my current travails.

But for the first time in my life, my heart and mind sang two different tunes. My steely mind bowed before a heavy heart as 10 years of life spent in building PCL flashed before my eyes.

As scene upon scene whirled before me, some in painfully slow motion, I felt as if time itself had come to a standstill. I didn't know what to make of the wild jumble of emotions that I found welling up inside.

But the mind, which had for so long pulled the heart along with it, wasn't to remain subservient to a grieving heart for so long and I soon found myself dissecting why things had come to such a pass.

I knew Dadan as well as he knew me and, as I stared at the ceiling, I was jolted by a sudden thought. Did Dadan hide some secrets in his heart that none of us knew? The more I thought of it, the more I was convinced that I was missing an important piece in the puzzle. The picture somehow seemed incomplete.

This time around, I played out my 10 years in a deliberate slow roll, hunting for clues, but I found none to match the missing puzzle piece. The mystery was as dark as the night surrounded me, but one of Dadan's often repeated statements refused to die away.

'*Dasgupta Seth, hum ko bara aadmi ban-na hai* (We have to be really big one day!)'

Did something lie behind the innocuous ambition statement, I wondered.

Twenty-two

I WOKE UP TO A BRIGHT and cheerful morning. It was going to be an eventful day and as providence would have, it was the last day of IT Asia '94.

As the chairman of IT Asia '94, I had called the mandatory press conference to mark the successful end of the marquee event and was welcomed by a packed house of reporters. We spoke of the numbers that made IT Asia '94 an even grander success than IT Asia '93.

We had attracted a footfall of over 200,000 business persons and had seen over 200 Indian and international companies participating. Most of the world's IT companies, with the exception of HP, had chosen to make their presence felt here. Some of the smaller companies had amassed over 2,000 enquiries, enough to last them through the year.

I thanked my colleagues at MAIT and specifically my erudite band of peers who had reposed faith in my vision. 'Going forward,' I said, 'IT Asia would turn out to be an even greater crowd-puller and the day is not far when the Indian IT industry would be reckoned as a global powerhouse.'

As the flow of the questions from the press corps ebbed, I threw in the biggest surprise of the evening and announced my stepping down from my role at PCL. 'I am doing this,' I remember saying, 'purely for personal reasons and in pursuit of my dreams. I have no doubt that PCL will continue to grow from strength to strength—an individual is but a mere speck in the larger scheme of things.'

I did not take any more questions as I chose to walk away from the limelight and into the unknown at the peak of my career and fame.

It felt good after a long time. Stepping away from the limelight, I realised, felt like a fresh breath of air against my face. There was no more proving to be done and I was free to follow the dictates of my soul—the excitement of diving into the unknown tugging at my heart.

The title of your memoir reminds me of Colonel Pickering congratulating Professor Higgins in *My Fair Lady* by singing, *'You did it, you said you would do it and did you did.'*

You also did it your way. For instance, you said you would get the Dell business for manufacturing motherboards in India and you did it. It was a folklore during those days when export of IT hardware services were unimaginable.

As a friend and a well-wisher, I have watched you diversifying into many new and disruptive areas with the same aplomb and being successful in that.

BDG, in all these you have had time for family (I hope Ranjana agrees) and friends. Teaming up with Pradeep Kar and Pravin Gandhi, the three of you set up a fabulous social network...BAIT, a platform that we and our families enjoyed. I hope it finds mention in your book.

Krish Vijayaraghavan
(Former chairman and MD, Advanced Micronic Devices)

The core Bengali Association Team, Vizag (1976).
From left, top row: Gautam, Bapi, Butu, Manas.
From left, bottom row: Snehamay, Bikram, Ratan Pal, Chottoraj

Nonagon (2016). From left: Siddhartha, Hitendu, Bikram, Shyamal, Apurba, Bidhu, Hazra

Bikram essays the lead role in one of the many plays staged by the Bengali Association Club in Vizag (1976)

Fellow IITian and Bikram's dear friend Abhindra

The Pink Elephant Restaurant in Vizag (1975)

Entrepreneur Sohan Hatangadi in Vizag (1975)

Snehamay Nag is flanked by Bikram and Bikram's wife Ranjana in Kolkata (earlier Calcutta) in 2016

Ranjana and Bikram Dasgupta—39 years and going strong

The PCL unbeatables.
From left: Bikram, Anil Bhushan Chopra,
Dadan Bhai, Bharat Goenka and Stephen Aranha (1989)

PCL's Bikram seals the historic $50-million deal with Dell in Austin, Texas,
for the manufacture of motherboards in India (1991)

Bikram with the Dell team in Austin, Texas (1991)

PCL–Dell Press Conference.
Andrew Harris, Executive VP, Dell, at the podium.
Looking on from left: David Beasley (Dell USA),
Bikram Dasgupta, Dadan Bhai, Anil Bhushan Chopra (1992)

Bikram's dear friend, A.B. Chopra, Director, PCL,
who was famously known as the 'ABC' of computer sales

Bikram performs a puja at the inaugural ceremony of
PCL's first corporate office in New Delhi (1992)

Off to Goa! Bikram's PCL team ready for departure at the Bombay airport (1989)

Bikram and his colleagues at a PCL picnic

Flying Solo

One

I WAS FINALLY AT PEACE WITH MYSELF and the world, and slept like an exhausted child who had had a rough night.

The serenity of facing up to your own fears and still darker trepidations to finally winning the battle, as much with the heart as with the mind, was an incomparable feeling. The ability to walk away from it all—name, fame and money—without looking back did not come easy. But a strong self-belief system married to a steely resolve of not letting go of one's most prized asset—one's value system—helped me put down the heavy baggage that I carried and walk away from it.

My decision to step down from PCL came as a shock to most. The press corps went into a frenzy clamouring for a sound bite, but I wasn't going to wash dirty linen in public. My team at PCL, however, were left at a loss by my sudden departure and I found the lane leading to my house awash with a sea of motorbikes and scooters the next evening.

The guys, most of them in their late 20s and early 30s, made up the core of PCL's aggressive sales force in north India and, emotionally charged as they were, they vowed to follow me into my new venture even if that meant going without any salary for a few months.

It touched my heart to see such adoration and I told them the only truth that I knew: 'I myself don't know what I am going to do next, guys. I need some time and space to sort things out.'

'But,' I continued, 'I know what you guys should do. All of you—and I mean all of you—should get back to doing what you do best. Do nothing that will harm PCL or shake us from our No. 1 spot in the market. One individual, however you might miss him or her, should not become the cause of your disenchantment. PCL is a great company and will continue to be so and needs your support now more than ever. I will always have you guys in my prayers and wish the best for you.'

Not that the guys were fully convinced, but I had left them with the only choice that I knew, that was the best for them and PCL. Nothing, I told myself, comes from hate or rancour and I vowed not to create a competitor to PCL—the lowest hanging fruit at my disposal.

There were a lot of drooping shoulders that day and it pained me to see it so, but there was scarcely anything that I could do. Some of the brighter lads though ended up working for me some years later when PCL suddenly found itself in a deep financial mess and had to finally go into dissolution.

As for Dadan Bhai, I didn't quite know what he made of my sudden departure. There were two facets of Dadan Bhai that I saw and I chose to remember the Dadan Bhai of yore—the fun-loving, ever-humming man with half his shirt buttons undone, and his unruly mop of hair hurriedly patted into place. He carried about him an ambition that was infectious, inspiring all who came in touch with him.

I loved him. He had changed my life, helping me discover myself and it has always remained that way for me.

~

Two

I SUDDENLY FOUND MYSELF UPROOTED from the familiarity of life that I had known and come to love. The thought of leaving PCL had never occurred to me. One does not leave one's family and PCL had been one big extended family. 'What do I do?' was a question that hung itself before me.

I had no answers and it vexed me greatly. The decision to quit PCL was so unforeseen that it did not leave me with any opportunity to plan for the future. I knew I wouldn't get into the IT hardware business—the only business I knew—but beyond that was the empty space of the universe.

Not one to brood over the past, I gathered my wits and set up my first firm, Global Synergies Ltd, and had it based out of New Delhi. I wasn't keen on joining a corporation, though the news that I was out in the market prompted calls from Sony Entertainment, Microsoft India, HCL and a couple of other well-known brands. All of them offered handsome salaries, excellent perks, equity stakes and the like on a platter—very tempting for a forty-year-old who found himself suddenly out of work—but I just wasn't ready to give up on my entrepreneurial urges.

'You are being foolhardy, Bikram. Take up the best offer,' the saner part of my brain admonished me, but the wilder and more vociferous part of my brain soon came rushing in, chiding, 'Don't be silly, Bikram. It is the unknown that holds the most promise!'

In the midst of all manner of calls offering me coveted jobs, I also landed some serious consulting offers. Having never professionally consulted before, I found the prospect somewhat exciting and made up my mind to focus on select consulting assignments until I came up with a viable and exciting project opportunity—something that I could leave my mark on.

A majority of the consulting offers came from very high net-worth businessmen who had made their fortunes in trading. With their sons returning from their studies abroad (most of them ended up attending some nondescript university), they found it difficult to assimilate their children into the daily rigours of business life.

Most of them readily believed that a highly branded professional in their midst could help rein in their wayward wards and they were ready to pay up to ₹5 lakh a day, back in 1994, if I were to choose to take up the offer and spend two or three days a month with them.

Taming a rich man's ward did not present itself as a relishing prospect and I continued sifting through the offers until I discovered two that looked somewhat promising.

The first involved helping a well-established industrialist set up a multi-layer Printed Circuit Board (PCB) plant. The gentleman had set his sights on manufacturing 42-layer PCBs, which was a highly sophisticated process those days, and it seemed a good project to involve myself with.

I knew a great deal about multi-layer PCBs, but a 42-layer PCB was an entirely different kettle of fish and exciting. These extremely sophisticated PCBs were used to run powerful computers, for instance, the Fujitsu M-780, a mainframe computer, and CDC ETA-10, again a multiprocessor mainframe machine that supported up to eight CPUs. The complex PCBs didn't come cheap and cost upwards of $10,000 apiece to manufacture during its early days.

Having acquainted myself with the technology, I gave the gentleman a broad plan and negotiated a fee of ₹5 lakh a day and proposed to present myself for one day each week, netting me a healthy ₹20 lakh a month—a handsome sum even by today's standards.

For the second assignment, I decided to forgo my monetary fees and instead fulfil a long-held aspiration. By the time I started consulting for the corporation, I had been handed over the keys to a mint-new BMW car—a long-cherished dream. The owners were only too pleased to accede to my request, happily accounting for the car as a capital purchase while availing of the handsome depreciation benefits in their books.

Life trudged on as I shuffled between fulfilling my consulting assignments and ferreting for projects that would excite me. I didn't enjoy the consulting assignments and was generally unhappy with the progress of things.

I came to the realisation that money could never make one happy, not at least the creative sort of person that I was. Money died fast. Sure, you did want the green bucks pouring in, but once you laid your hands on them, there was only so much that one could do with material things and they, too, died on you.

There was also a second facet to money. With the kind of money that I was commanding in the market, guys who dipped into their pockets tended to treat persons like pieces of turd and almost controlled their lives. I was lucky on that front since bestowed with high brand equity and a temper to match, people didn't dare cross the line with me. But it was not an experience one could tom-tom about.

It was about this time that I happened to receive a request from the managing director of Webel (West Bengal Electronics Industry Development Corporation), a government of West Bengal enterprise, inviting me to present a talk at their showcase Gateway '95 electronics exhibition. I was requested to meet some senior officials of Webel at their office in Hauz Khas, New Delhi, to help chalk things out.

The senior officials of Webel, who were then stationed in New Delhi, implored me to base my new venture in Bengal. As fellow Bengalis, they thought it would be an edifying moment if a celebrated son of the soil could return to the land of his ancestors and start life anew. I remained non-committal and reiterated to my audience that I had yet to find myself a project that could get me excited enough to throw myself fully into it.

It was in February of 1995 that I landed back in Calcutta after a hiatus of more than a decade. Calcutta looked the same to me. Long tree-lined boulevards suddenly getting pinched into narrow traffic-infested streets. Trams were still rattling down busy thoroughfares, their faint bells drowned by the roar of speeding buses in their bid to engorge themselves with passengers until they seemed to stretch the very seams of the rickety carriages. History lived cheek by jowl with protruding modern edifices.

'Calcutta remains the same old Calcutta; stuck in history, fighting with itself to cling on to its own distinctive sapidity,' I thought; a city that you can't help but fall in love with. One that never seems far from your thoughts, however distant you might have moved or travelled the world.

I was affectionately welcomed by Mr Nandan Bhattacharya, the managing director of Webel, and introduced to a galaxy of personalities who had made it to the exhibition. It included Partha Sarathi Ghosh of Boston Pledge, a well-known policy adviser and strategist for corporates and governments and an innovator of business and economic models. The Bengal government had done their homework in right earnest.

To my disappointment, I was slotted to be the last speaker—a slot that I assiduously avoided. That I was not very well known in Bengal, my home state, was evident. It was a state that had perfected the art of running into itself and figured low down in all industrial development indices.

It was evening by the time I got my opportunity to take to the stage, the audience discernibly exhausted by the barrage of presentations that preceded me.

I chose not to beam my presentation and instead elected to speak impromptu. After the customary thanking of the dignitaries, I looked at the audience and paused awhile, adding to the mystery of a high-flying Bengali from New Delhi who had come to Calcutta to address the crowd.

'Ladies and gentlemen,' I said, leaning suggestively into the microphone, 'I had diligently prepared a 12-slide presentation for the evening, but as luck would have it, each speaker took away two slides and my friend, the last speaker, has managed to walk away with the last three slides, including the "thank you" slide, and here I am before you bereft of a presentation.'

The audience burst into laughter, and thus jolted from their evening torpor, gave me an opportunity to speak my mind. I spoke about the potential of Bengal and the promise of its youth. I told them about my love for Nike's tagline 'Just do it'. Bengal's youth, I exhorted, were endowed with both intellect and passion, but lacked the final push to ford the unknown and 'Just do it'.

The audience, to my surprise and relief, took well to my speech and by the time I was done, I found myself surrounded by people eager to have a word with me.

Nandan da, noticing my predicament, rescued me from the clutches of the crowd and taking me aside, said, 'Do something in Bengal, Bikram.'

'But I am returning to Delhi tonight and I am still undecided on my next move, Nandan da,' I responded.

'Very well,' said Nandan da, 'I shall be in Delhi next week with all my directors. Come over and spend an evening with us and we can have a serious chat...' and taking me by my shoulders, walked me to the dining area, saying, 'Enough of talking, come let's get our stomachs something to celebrate tonight.'

Nandan da always carried a furious sense of humour.

Dada, as I have known him, has always been a big thinker and a great executioner of big ideas. The deal with Dell is an example of that.

He was a great believer in creating brands and he continues doing that in his new ventures post PCL.

I had met him during the PCL days and while I had no business dealings with him, I was impressed with his salesmanship. Here was a guy, very charming and yet an aggressive sales person.

We have been friends ever since. I consider it a privilege to have known him and Ranjana as friends.

Honest, well-meaning and a good human being.

Pravin Gandhi
(Former chairman and co-founder Hindtron; former director, Digital Equipment Corp.; entrepreneur, investor, philanthropist and an icon of the Indian IT industry)

Three

I DON'T RECOLLECT IF I MET Nandan Bhattacharya and his team of directors at a restaurant or a club; it was most likely a club, frequented by Indian Administrative Service cadre officers, since I remember shaking hands with a few bureaucrats whom I had come to know during my PCL days.

Nandan da had chosen a relaxed environment for the evening and as we sat cradling our whiskys, he explained how Webel was planning to set up an intelligent building in the upcoming electronics hub at Salt Lake, on the north-eastern fringes of Calcutta. 'We have already earmarked the land for the project, but…' and he let the sentence trail off in the air before adding, 'the project should be ready in two to three years.'

'Pretty high-vaulting dream,' I thought, as my mind raced back to my days at the Indian Oxygen factory, where I had witnessed how the gas regulator guys chose to play cards, while chomping on omelette sandwiches, instead of repairing a single additional regulator beyond their allocated quota even if that meant taking home some extra money. That was Bengal then, home to the demurring but passionately trade unionist worker.

But Nandan da was dead serious. 'Bikram,' he said, shaking me from my reverie, 'why don't you set up a software factory in the upcoming building? I will be more than happy to give you an entire floor of 10,000 square feet, and Webel shall take a 20 per cent equity stake in your new company in lieu of it. You will also have the freedom to buy back your shares once you get fully up and running.'

I gave the proposal some thought as I slowly sipped my whisky, a perfectly aged single malt. It sounded pretty enticing and to get an entire floor virtually for free was not a bad idea.

'Nandan da,' I said, looking into his eyes, 'one floor is too small for me. I would like to have the whole building.'

Nandan Bhattacharya went wide-eyed and for a moment didn't believe his ears. Turning to the attendant standing next to him, he bellowed, 'Hand me a stiff whisky, will you? Good lord! What is this young man talking?'

Drink in hand, Nandan da turned his attention to me and said, 'Now, Bikram, tell me exactly what do you have in mind?'

'With all due respect to you and your colleagues here,' I said, 'one floor wouldn't suit my style nor my temperament. I would need the whole project. I shall build you a futuristic intelligent building. You must trust me enough to leave its conception and execution to me. I will raise money for the project, brand and market the project and sell it. You needn't lift a finger except to hand over the land to a joint venture company that we can form and you can also take a 20 per cent equity stake in the JV.'

Nandan da heard me out fully, but it was his turn to be non-committal. 'I can't take such a decision independently. I am, after all, a part of the government machinery and it's only the government that can take such decisions,' he said, before we turned our attention to dinner.

It was for the second time that month that I found myself on a flight to Calcutta. As the pilot touched down to a near perfect landing, I had, for the second time after my Dell deal, found the abiding truth in John F. Kennedy's famous lines: 'Let us never negotiate out of fear. But let us never fear to negotiate.'

It was an axiom that I truly believe in. Some people though chose to see it as my penchant for brinkmanship.

Nandan Bhattacharya called me a few days later with some good news. 'Bikram,' he said, 'Mr Somnath Chatterjee is keen to hear from you about your taking up the project that we spoke about. I have fixed a one-on-one meeting with him. Should you be able to convince him, we shall only have to have the chief minister's nod to go ahead.'

I met Nandan da on the steps of Writers' Building. As we trooped down the hallway, Nandan da briefed me about his previous meetings with Somnath babu, as he was affectionately called, and fished out the official memo that he had written to the powerful minister and a close confidant of Jyoti Basu, the Leftist chief minister of West Bengal.

Somnath Chatterjee came from an illustrious family. His father Nirmal Chandra Chatterjee was a prominent lawyer, intellectual, and Hindu revivalist and nationalist around the time of India's independence. Nirmal Chandra Chatterjee formed the All India Civil Liberties Council and agitated for the release of the members of the Communist Party of India, which had been banned by India's first prime minister, Jawaharlal Nehru. In the process, Chatterjee became close to Jyoti Basu in spite of their ideological and political differences.

This time around, I had done my homework well and soon had Somnath babu eagerly participating in an animated discussion about my vision of the futuristic intelligent building that I had proposed.

'I suggest that we name the project Infinity—one with infinite possibilities,' I said in response to Nandan da's question on what should be name of the project. The name resounded well with my audience and has stuck since.

'I don't see it as a mere building or an infrastructure project, sirs,' I told Somnath babu and Nandan da, 'but as a beacon of change for a new Bengal. I believe that with Infinity, we shall claim our rightful place in the IT map of India, and Bengal will again be a harbinger of profound change in how we look at creating work environments for a whole new generation of technology workers.'

A few weeks later, I was sitting with the chief minister, Jyoti Basu, reiterating my vision for IT in Bengal and making Infinity a cornerstone of this vision. Accompanied by Somnath babu and Nandan da, both of whom batted for the project, Mr Basu gave his nod to go ahead with our plans.

Thus was born Infinity, India's first truly intelligent workplace. Sporting, for the first time, a true 'plug-and-play' infrastructure, it was the precursor to IT parks in India.

⌒∽⌒

Four

Back in new delhi, I got a call from Shiv Nadar's office, saying that he wanted to meet me.

I met Shiv over lunch in his private dining room at an office. The man always did things in style and one couldn't help but feel honoured by being in his presence. Shiv's style was another facet of his brilliant mind—one that shone through as you spoke to him.

'What are you up to now, Bikram?' he asked.

'Nothing much...still at the loose end of things,' I replied, smiling.

'Very well,' responded Shiv. 'I have identified a role for you.'

He then proceeded to offer me the opportunity of strategically managing three of his companies—HCL Consulting, HCL Technologies and one other that I am finding it difficult to recall.

'You will be sitting next to me and managing these three entities for me, Bikram, as I gradually transit out from them. We will start with sweat equity and as you build your reserves, you can plough back some to buy up to 24 per cent stake in each of these entities,' he proposed.

I was taken by surprise. It was an enormously impressive offer and it sent my mind racing. I paused for a moment and dipped into my bag to fish out the still warm contract that I had signed with the West Bengal government and pushed it across to him.

Shiv gave the document a good read and pushing the paper back to me said, 'But you have already committed yourself!'

'Sort of,' I replied.

'No, Bikram. You should honour this contract. It is from your home state and the government has reposed a lot of faith and trust in you by putting their seal on this contract. I will get people or maybe I will not, but this is a big honour and you shouldn't let them down. I bless you and my best wishes shall always be with you.' Saying so, he closed the chapter and happily tucked into his lunch.

As I walked away from that lunch, I realised that every time I had met Shiv Nadar, I stepped out with something extremely valuable from him. Such men are a rarity nowadays.

◆

My mind firmly on the Infinity project, I took the next flight to Singapore. I wanted to see the workings of an 'intelligent' building from the inside out and India didn't have any. I also had one more agenda that needed to be ticked off.

During that tour of Singapore, I realised what Lee Kuan Yew, the nation's founding father and premier from 1959 to 1990, had achieved. I now appreciated the purport of what Singaporeans meant when they proudly declared that Lee Kuan Yew had, in a single generation, transited the country from the Third World to the First World.

Few Third World leaders had the foresight of Lee Kuan Yew to bring in First World infrastructure to attract Japanese, American and European entrepreneurs to set up their bases in Singapore, and by the 1980s, the city state had managed to emerge as a major electronics exporter—something that we had heavily tapped into during my days at PCL. I now saw the real development behind the electronics screen.

During that visit, Singapore graciously dipped into her hamper and gave me a rich pool of ideas and access to globally recognised resources and professionals for my idea of Infinity.

Study tour over, I focused on my second Singaporean agenda.

Ravinder Chamaria, my nemesis for what was supposed to be my watershed Russian computer deal, was pleasantly startled to see his secretary ushering me into his office. 'What brings you to Singapore, Mr Dasgupta?' he asked, not even trying to hide his surprise.

'Won't you tell me to take a seat?' I quipped back with a smile, extending my hand to him.

I had kept my promise, made almost half a decade ago, of giving him a call the day I left PCL, and Mr Chamaria in his exuberance had promised me up to ₹5 crore in 72 hours, as an investment fund, if I ever needed it with no strings attached or questions asked.

The creative part of me felt somewhat Shylockian to present myself thus at Mr Chamaria's office, but business prudence prevailed and I felt at ease after a while of chatting with him.

A sharp businessman that he was, Mr Chamaria must have intuited the reason for my sudden appearance, but waited for me to fire the first salvo. A good angler, having dangled a juicy bait, is but a picture of patience.

'Mr Chamaria, I have signed a contract with the West Bengal government to help build India's first intelligent workplace and I am out raising funds for this one-of-its-kind project. You are the first person that came to mind and besides you have a date with a well-aged commitment,' I said, giving him my brightest smile.

'Sure, a commitment is a commitment, sir. So, how much do you need?' he asked.

'The whole of the 5 crore that you promised,' I responded.

'*Abhi chahiye kya?* (Do you want it right away?)' asked Mr Chamaria, looking incredulously at me.

'*Aap bol doh* (Give me your word) and it's enough for me,' I said, sounding gracious.

My benefactor hadn't expected me to arrive so soon at his door to make good of his promise and found himself to be somewhat at a loss to put together the monies that I was looking for. He remained silent, engrossed deep in thought, before saying, 'Let's work on this. We will figure out something.'

༄

Five

With the infinity project signed up, I gave up on the sporadic consulting assignments and found myself shifting base to Calcutta for the second time in my life.

The decision to move to Calcutta didn't come easy. It was in New Delhi that I had earned my spurs—a region that had feted me and I, in turn, had grown both professionally and personally.

But if I wanted people to believe in the gradual industrial revival of Bengal, I had to be personally seen to be reposing faith and acting on my own dictums. Additionally, one couldn't manage a project of the ambition and scale of Infinity sitting in faraway New Delhi, wielding a remote control.

I made a second visit to Singapore, armed with the new knowledge that I had gleaned from my last visit. This time around, my contacts in Singapore helped put me in touch with a number of top-notch construction and architectural firms, among which Singapore Technologies Construction Pte Ltd, one of Southeast Asia's largest high-tech construction and multi-disciplinary companies, figured prominently on the list.

Back in Calcutta, in 1995, we formed Globsyn Webel Ltd as the JV company where 20 per cent of the stake was held by Webel and the balance by Global Synergies Ltd, which now went under the Globsyn nomenclature. We also managed to rope in Singapore Technologies Construction (Sembcorp Construction now) as the lead consultants for the project—their first project as lead consultants in India.

Infinity became an obsession for me. I could think of nothing except creating an infrastructure that went beyond the mere boundaries of computer-integrated buildings, itself an emerging technology in India.

My final vision of Infinity encompassed a fully integrated complex with twin twenty-two-storeyed intelli-centres, providing 8,00,000 square feet of 'plug-and-play' workplace at the centrepiece of the edifice. I did not stop at that and planned ahead for some 1,200 intelli-homes, each sporting a global connectivity terminal linked to the workplace, for professionals working in high-end and niche technology areas.

By the time I was done with putting the final touches to the plans for my dream project, the total cost stood at an astounding ₹350 crore and an infrastructure spread over 40 acres of virgin marshland.

Money never worried me. Money, I believed, could always be raised and wouldn't be an insurmountable barrier for as ambitious a project as Infinity. But I was to be proved wrong some years down the line. It had not so much to do with raising money (it was easy), but it was who one took it from and their appreciation of the project's vision.

Not knowing anything about construction or architecture didn't bother me in the least and I managed to get on board some of the best minds in the business either as employees or consultants, and each day turned out to be a new exercise in learning.

But I armed myself with sufficient knowledge on building automation, something that I found extremely interesting.

As the construction progressed, it almost became a ritual for me to drive down, in the dead of the night, through the desolate, dimly lit streets of Salt Lake to see the steadily rising concrete-and-steel structure. Parking my car at the edge of the project site, I would watch in fascination as workers milled around the structure like an army of gigantic worker ants, clambering up the steel-and-iron scaffoldings, yellow helmets glistening under the harsh light of the floodlights that lit up the place, throwing long, eerily human-like shadows.

I felt a magical thrill coursing through my veins as I saw the structure going up, as if to kiss the very skies. To me, Infinity was a living and breathing organism, one that seemed to have a life of its very own, and I had to check myself from talking back to it.

As the months rolled into years, I stared at the dwindling bank accounts, wondering where the next tranche of money would come from. Banks were of little use and would only mean a waste of time. I needed a financier who could bankroll the project before work came to a dead halt.

The only time that I felt at peace during those days came from my nightly sojourns to the project site as the towers stood up majestically against the ground, getting ready to be clad in shiny glass cladding. To me, the exterior cladding seemed like a bride's wedding trousseau as they shone and sparked against the moonlit sky.

My search for a financier again landed me at the doors of Mr Chamaria, who was only eager to throw in a lifeline in exchange for an equity stake against his investments.

Money came and money died, but with it went my vision of what Infinity should really have been. To Mr Chamaria, Infinity was a superlative real estate project in the midst of a realty boom in Calcutta and he treated it as so.

To have grudged him for his thinking was perhaps off beam, something that I realised many years later. For him, technology held little importance in the face of the order of square footage that he had to sell to recover his investment at market-rate returns. Technology only helped in gaining an invaluable bargaining toehold. He was perhaps more practical and rooted in the brutal truths of life than I was.

At times, I felt like my mentor Arjun Malhotra and Shiv Nadar; swayed by the passion of building a technology-laced edifice and an all-consuming fire to create a differentiator. To this was added the 'all-for-results' Dadan Bhai and creating a fiery edifice.

But history always has a way of viewing things differently and maybe both Mr Chamaria and I were equally correct in our views, given the different prisms that we were holding to our eyes.

∽

Six

WHILE THE INFINITY PROJECT was well underway, I still carried the feeling of 'rootlessness' within me. I had to look at life beyond 'Infinity', which increasingly came to be seen as a pure-play real estate project despite my own conviction that I was building an edifice for the knowledge worker of the 21st century.

By 1997–98, I was being invited by various state governments to speak on the subject of intelligent infrastructure. Almost all of them welcomed my ideas with open arms, but fell prey to viewing such projects as new-age real estate plays to attract investors to their individual states. I didn't see myself as a real estate player and was happy to walk away after sharing my ideas.

In the midst of all this, I watched in fascination two gigantic waves that promised to change the face of the IT industry in India. The first was the steady growth in ferrying software engineers from India to prime offshore locations in the US and UK as well as Europe to some limited degree. This came to be known by the unkindest of terms—'body shopping'—and went on to become the revenue bulwark, during those formative years, for most of the large IT companies today.

The second lay in the spurt of institutes that trained graduates, largely urban youth from non-science backgrounds with a bright aptitude, in information technology including programming techniques on technologies that ruled the roost during that time.

I saw promise in both these developments. To me, 'body shopping' stood at the lowest end of the value chain; sure it raked in a sackful of green bucks, but given the brightness and ingenuity of Indian engineers, the country and its IT firms could offer a much richer basket of services should the engineers be geared for it.

Second, I clung to my view that mass training unsupported by appropriate pedagogical interventions diluted the very essence of creating truly 'industry ready' professionals—a view that some found to be somewhat stodgy during that time.

It was these twin streams of thought that first gave me the idea of forming India's first and perhaps only software finishing school till date. To me, a software finishing school was much beyond pure technology training and encompassed critical work and life skills interventions along with skilling people on basic managerial aspects; aspects that resonated with managing oneself in the new and emerging knowledge-driven economy—one that was to be termed as the 'knowledge economy' some years down the line.

Once struck, the idea grew on me to a point of restlessness. My instincts told me that I had hit upon a brilliant proposition and all that remained was bouncing my idea off my friends in the industry. Their vetting would turn out to be critical if I had to gain any kind of real traction against some of the strongest and largest players in the industry.

Almost all my friends found great merit in my proposition, but were unsure if such an idea could be pulled off in a market that was infested with quick-fix solutions and hole-in-the-wall training outfits. Also, the big boys, such as NIIT Aptech and their like, could well pose to be formidable opponents unless I managed to pull myself away from their gravitational sphere.

Given the hard baking that I had gone through at HCL and PCL, I wasn't overly worried about competition, but then I needed something that could literally pull me away from the sphere of normal training outfits.

Armed with the idea of the software finishing school, I chose to visit Singapore again. This time, my destination was IBM. With 70 per cent of the world's data residing on IBM machines, approaching them seemed to be the only natural progression in my quest for an enduring market differentiator.

My timing proved to be propitious since IBM was, around that time, investigating possible pathways to make its first foray into the fast-growing software space in India and found in me and my idea of a software finishing school a fortuitous vehicle to carry their brand. It was a win-win deal for both sides and I walked away a happy man.

Back in town, my search for a dedicated campus to house my software finishing school brought me to an abandoned monitor manufacturing factory of the G.P. Goenka Group. Spread over some two-and-a-half acres, the site was a few blocks away from Infinity and came with a readily done-up building that could do with some modifications.

IBM had been generous with me and opened their purse strings to extend a soft loan of $1,30,000 based purely on the conviction and passion that drove my dreams and some well-done presentations. This was a huge leg-up for an unknown fledgling start-up like mine and gave me a huge high.

In addition, my deal with IBM helped me get, at fairly discounted rates, an IBM S/390 mainframe, an AS-400 server and 96 node computers with IBM executing the entire network cabling exercise themselves.

But the biggest coup in my deal with IBM lay in persuading their management, led by Mike Colleary, director, China/Hong Kong, to lend their coveted 'IBM' brand name to my software finishing school. Thus was born the IBM Centre for Software Excellence, the only kind of its institution in the whole of South Asia with IBM stamped all over it.

By 1998, when West Bengal Chief Minister Jyoti Basu inaugurated TechnoCampus (the brand name for the software finishing school and its campus), we were ready with a six-month IBM-certified course supported by an IBM-trained faculty pool.

With the world poised at the cusp of transiting its business applications to be Y2K-ready (year 2000 date format-compliant), our six-month programme, based on an innovative pedagogical approach, was designed to impart students a rigorous 'back-to-school' training experience in Y2K solution/patch development, web application development using Java, Lotus Domino/Notes application development, database management on IBM mainframes, transaction-oriented application development and AS/400 application development.

So started anew another fervent journey, in the form of Globsyn in 1997, carrying forward the passion that I had felt at PCL.

There can be only one Bikram da!

What is a good barometer of success? I imagine it would be a person like Bikram Dasgupta, who has been a pioneer in the Indian information technology industry with a voracious appetite for creating ideas, building relationships, nurturing talent, growing businesses and bringing tons of happiness to those around him. Today, he stands tall as a thinker, a first-generation entrepreneur and a master risk-taker. He is confident, popular and hasn't shown signs of slowing down. To me, he is the very essence of 'cool'. If Bikram da (as he is called) was a Facebook post, he would have drawn a record-breaking number of 'Likes'.

I first met Bikram da in 1986, during a stint with Computer Point. He was with Pertech Computers Ltd (PCL) and had launched their PCs. We were discussing the idea of selling his PCs through Computer Point. But, during our conversation, he just couldn't resist offering me a job. Who knows what path I would have taken had I taken up his offer...

In 1994, we co-founded the Beer Drinkers Association of Information Technology (BAIT) along with Pravin Gandhi. In his wisdom, Bikram da realised that an informal organisation like BAIT could help solve many problems for all of us without the intervention of an industry body.

BAIT resulted in many business issues being resolved between leaders of the IT industry with the bonus of several friendships being forged when we met over beer. A lasting one emerged with Bikram da and his family.

Bikram da was (and is) a visionary. He had seen the PC revolution way ahead of others and had signed a $50 million deal for manufacturing computer motherboards with Michael Dell. Remember, this was in the 1990s, when we were barely conversant with electronic typewriters.

He went on to create Infinity in Kolkata, one of the first tech parks in the country—once more, way ahead of others. This was followed by a string of ventures like the ultra-modern Globsyn Business School. He knew that India would need a steady supply of top-notch executive talent and a new generation of engineers. But more than this, it was his deeply passionate approach to people that drove him to set up the school. He wanted everyone to realise their true potential.

Somewhere in between his hectic schedules, he almost set up a very successful Mexican food chain. Most would relate this to his being a food-loving Bengali. And they would not be wrong. But it goes deeper than a love of food. Bikram da is curious by nature; he wants to experiment and innovate, and he will not stop until he has done things his way.

I join my wife Kalpana in wishing Bikram da the very best in the journey that lies ahead and may he never run out of wind in his sails.

Pradeep Kar
(Chairman and MD, Microland Ltd)

Seven

I HAVE ALWAYS BEEN FORTUITOUS when it came to people, and in my solo flight, I found in Professor Biswajit Nag a well-wisher and technology mentor for life.

Professor Nag was counted among the pioneers in the field of computer science and engineering, and had helped in building the Atlas Computer (a second-generation machine, using discrete germanium transistors; a joint development between the University of Manchester, Ferranti and Plessey) and the ISIJU computer at the Jadavpur University in 1966, one of the first indigenous efforts in building a solid-state second-generation computer.

During his ten-year long tenure as the director of IIT Bombay, Professor Nag helped build a strong faculty, particularly in the computer science and engineering departments, an aspect that was to prove of invaluable help during my setting up of the faculty pool at Globsyn TechnoCampus.

A warm and effusive person, Professor Nag readily agreed to chair the TechnoCampus academic council and his pride showed through in his interactions with the media during the inauguration of the TechnoCampus, where he stated, '...it was apt that Calcutta would host a unique training centre like TechnoCampus since the Indian Statistical Institute hosted the country's first computer in the city and the Jadavpur University introduced university-level computer education in the country.'

With TechnoCampus up and running, we were on a roll, growing at more than 100 per cent each year. There is nothing like tasting success and it stoked my fiery ambitions further.

It gave me a certain sense of invincibility as I saw my students getting drafted into plum jobs in almost all of India's leading IT companies and

I was deluged with stories of success. It was during this time that we launched our Young Software Manager (YSM) programme.

This time around, I moved away from the confines of IBM-driven technologies and created a truly holistic IT training programme—one that concentrated on all major and emerging technologies, apart from bringing in critical management and life skills into the curriculum's ambit.

Our IBM experience proved invaluable in refining our pedagogical approach and the six-month YSM programme, priced at ₹85,000, proved to be a runaway success. We were raking in money by the fistful.

Meant only for non-computer science engineers and exceptionally bright graduates, YSM gave its participants a first-hand experience in the inner workings of an IT firm and enabled them to scramble up an organisation's hierarchy as they came armed with requisite managerial skills that were offered by none of the technology training institutions back then.

YSM was in many ways my part-answer, part-rebellion against the linearity of the Indian education system. The system did not align itself with market needs, while students bore the brunt of this yawning academia-industry divide, something that still plagues the system to some extent.

Back then, engineering students went through five long years of academic regimentation. With the area of study during the first three years being common to all students, they would be exposed to their subjects of choice only during the last two years of their engineering studies.

This long regimentation, I realised, did nothing in my search for creative software professionals; the kind of professionals, I came to believe, our country would need in ever large numbers if we were to globally make a mark in IT-enabled services.

Software engineering and programming was more about 'aptitude' than possessing 'knowledge'. Being armed with knowledge without possessing the right aptitude was a sure recipe for disaster.

This formed the core of the reasoning for our YSM programme and we made sure that candidates had the right 'aptitude'; knowledge was something as a subject that we could deal very well with.

This fundamental understanding opened up the floodgates for creative software programmers in India, giving access to a large but latent talent pool.

Buoyed by our success, we started opening centres modelled on TechnoCampus across the country, starting with New Delhi. Based on a highly reworked franchisee model, we sought out prospective partners with adequate infrastructure at prime city locations. The partners were offered a healthy share of the profits, while Globsyn controlled both the faculty pool as well as the delivery and quality mechanisms.

At the peak of our success with YSM, we ended up opening a centre in almost every quarter and YSM soon became a brand to be reckoned with. If we raked in money, we also invested heavily in marketing and building the brand.

We ran YSM advertisements nationwide across all popular dailies and were flooded with responses. We were envied for our marketing prowess and some of our advertisement copies stood out for their creativity and jargon-less communication, something that was drilled into me early in my career by none other than the stalwart Amit Dutta Gupta himself.

I remember one of our most enduring ads that went something like this...

'What do Disney's *Lion King*, Spielberg's dinosaurs, Michael Jackson's videos and your father's office have in common?' This we ran in a large and bold typeface and followed it up with the answer 'Computers' in a smaller typeface followed, in turn, by the rest of the body copy.

In some ways, we had changed how training outfits advertised those days and Globsyn's ads were always looked out for.

We devised our own entrance test that we developed in collaboration with the Indian Institute of Psychometry, Calcutta, and named it GSAT (Globsyn Software Aptitude Test). YSM had caught on the popular imagination and our end-season placements were the talk of the town. At our peak, we ran two batches at each of our centres and had ramped up our fees to ₹1 lakh—a pricing strategy that some of my industry friends had laughed at when I had run the plan past them.

We were chugging along at a furious pace when two cataclysmic events between 2000 and 2001 took the wind out of our sails and I suddenly found myself adrift again.

If YSM saw a huge spurt in our revenues, it also fuelled my investors' desire to cash in on the success and steadily besieged me with requests to take Globsyn public. We had a lot going for us those days. Apart from our training business, our software firm that specialised in IBM mainframe technologies, along with other emerging technologies, was working for some of the largest business brands in the US, bringing home useful dollars.

We had also devised an entirely new method in IT training delivery, combining a mix of online and instructor-led training where students were free to pursue their technology skills using a self-customised mix of both methods that gave them the liberty of pursuing their other vocations or part-time jobs. This we branded as 'Knowledge Pubs' and also invested heavily in building an online education platform.

◊

Eight

I KNEW NEXT TO NOTHING ABOUT taking a company public except for a limited experience in marketing the PCL IPO or initial public offering. I was finally persuaded by my investors to take the plunge in 2001 to disastrous consequences.

I relied heavily on outside wisdom, but felt weighed down by the kind of advice that came my way. I had always believed in playing by the rules and decided to ignore some of the more unnerving suggestions. I had always done things my way and I saw no reason to deviate from the time-tested path.

A creative person at heart, ideas sprouted much before commerce came to me, and I watched in dread as odious sums of money were sunk into the preparations that went into taking the company public. My instincts told me something was wrong with the world economic order showing traces of ominous dark clouds on the horizon, but my investors were gungho and we pushed for a hefty premium on our shares. With a face value of ₹10 per share, we were asking for a premium of ₹35–40 per share, something that my investors were confident was the right thing to do. Did the numbers add up? I thought they did, but I was to be proved wrong.

I was left with little choice but to play the game. I held firmly to my decision of not trying to game the system as I landed in Bombay, some 12 days before we were scheduled to go public, unaware of the catastrophe that was to unfold itself before me.

With a day to go before the launch, I read the newspapers with trepidation, with most analysts sowing seeds of doubt about the quantum of premium that we were asking for, when I received a call from one the lead bankers who were underwriting the issue. They were unceremoniously backing off from the issue, leaving me in a precarious situation.

I called a senior management official of the bank, only to hear the voice at the other end of the line say, 'Why are you calling me now? What has been done has been done and there is nothing that we can do. Thank you.' I had paid the ultimate price for not heeding the advice to take care of the 'system' within the system beforehand.

News like that, I realised, didn't stay under wraps for long in Maximum City and I soon found some deep-pocketed gentlemen offering to bail me out of my precarious situation. I turned down all such offers, unsure of what lurked behind the shadows.

I didn't know what to do or what my next move should be. It was as if my mind had gone into a rapid shutdown. It was a while before I woke up from my state of stupor and took one of the boldest decisions of my life.

'If I have done it my way all through, I will have it my way here also,' I thought as I steeled myself for the inevitable. With a few hours to go before the launch, I pulled out the issue, choosing instead the ignominy of refunding the IPO application money.

I returned to Calcutta the same night a shattered and broken man. It was inconceivable that an IPO from Bikram Dasgupta was pulled out at the last moment. But surprisingly enough, my friends in the media stood by me and heralded my bold decision. They commended me for not falling prey to the system. I hardly had time to recover from my IPO debacle when I was felled again by a massive blow—more hurting and devastating than the first.

By late 2000 and early 2001, the rapidly burgeoning internet industry came to be seen as a bubble. One that was not sustainable by any sane economic yardstick. To compound the matter, the Y2K scare had come and gone. The software engineers who had worked on the Y2K crisis ended up joining start-up internet companies by the droves.

I watched on in horror as the NASDAQ Composite Index started shedding points almost on a daily basis with our own bourses mirroring the trend. There was blood on the streets as over-valued dot com companies suddenly found themselves without the benevolent support of venture capitalists.

Everyone was losing money as companies started looking at their burnrates and found themselves eating into their existing capital. They were eating into themselves from the inside out and started shedding weight. Out went the ambitious marketing and advertisement spends quickly followed by mass layoffs.

Computer professionals, feted till just the other day for their technology expertise, suddenly found themselves on the streets, leading to a massive glut in the job market. Indian companies drew back thousands of their employees from their abandoned and fast sinking on-site internet projects.

Offshore projects, including some of our own, fared no better. Companies were scaling down their services as demand dropped at an alarming rate. It was a struggle for survival now. The euphoria surrounding the motto of 'get big fast' had finally managed to run into itself.

As if this weren't enough, the 11 September 2001 attack on the World Trade Center twin towers proved to be the proverbial final nail in the coffin. Global stock markets went into a downward spiral, hurting companies across the board. Giants such as CISCO lost up to 86 per cent of their market capitalisation.

Back home at Globsyn, we were hit with bad news almost on a weekly basis. Technology companies were suddenly awash with excess manpower and fresh hires were the first in line to feel the brunt of the catastrophe that was unfolding. As clients cut back on their projects, IT companies were left with little choice but to let go of their excess talent.

Nine

YSM TOOK THE HIT BADLY. It became a challenge to place the existing students in a lopsided supply-driven market. New admissions were a distant dream and we were left staring at rows of empty classrooms across all centres, including our mother centre in Calcutta.

As the wildfires raged on showing no signs of abating, we were left with no choice but to close down one centre after another. By the end of 2001, we were left with only the Calcutta TechnoCampus and a paltry seven students, down from a peak of more than 1,200, each paying ₹1 lakh during our heydays.

The IPO debacle, along with the sudden shrinking in the training and education market, affected my health badly. I found myself ageing disproportionately and this affected my whole being. I was going through the most trying phase of my life and I had hardly anyone to turn to except Ranjana, who stood like a rock beside me, with Rahul and Romit still in college in the US.

In the midst of all the turmoil I suffered, the most was to let some of my most brilliant people go. I was left with no other option. We had simply run out of cash.

We tried desperately to weather the storm and barely managed to keep our heads above the water as I saw firms of all sizes being dragged into the abyss. Firms of our size stood little chance and were swept away by the tide.

How does one cope with calamities of such magnitude? Is there a right or wrong approach to rowing in rough seas? Wouldn't it be wise to just shut shop and walk away with a bruised ego to fight another battle another day? Does one lose one's risk appetite in the face of the first signs of disaster? Shouldn't I be enjoying the unknown, something that

I felt so passionately about?

These and a myriad other thoughts consumed my day as I struggled to put together whatever cash I could to pay my remaining staff. For someone who took pride in paying well and on time, I found myself paying salaries sometimes in the middle of the month. In a large number of cases, my senior staff chose to take massive salary cuts so that their lesser-paid brethren could be paid from whatever fast dwindling cash that we had.

We were in the thick of the storm when it occurred to me that lying passive wouldn't do anyone any good. My people looked up to me to bail them out of the mess that we found ourselves in—something that we had little control over.

It was then that I thought about adding a floor to our only remaining campus in Calcutta. It was a maddening thought. Was I being foolish in exposing myself to a hefty credit line only to create more classrooms when the existing ones were sitting empty?

All my instincts told me that I would be able to fill my classrooms as I chided myself for losing faith in myself and announced my decision to the staff. My people didn't know how to react. Some must have walked away that evening feeling I had lost touch with reality, but they chose to stand by me.

So, in the midst of all the debris, the Calcutta TechnoCampus surrounded itself again in a mesh of scaffoldings. We were a sight to behold. It was as much a statement to the world that we were alive and kicking as it was to me to rebuild a business that had been battered by the storm.

In September 2002, we launched Globsyn Business School as India's first corporate business school. We were already running behind schedule, but managed to rope in 56 young persons to what was to be the maiden batch of Globsyn management graduates in a long line of batches to come.

For the first time since 2000, the dark clouds over our heads were showing signs of abating, but we weren't out of the woods yet. Our resilience seemed to be paying off.

Ten

YSM NEVER REALLY RECOVERED from the battering that it had received. The markets had changed in the aftermath of the storm and computer science as a subject came to be offered in almost all private and government-run engineering colleges, leading to a steep drop in interest for programmes such as YSM.

YSM limped along and we never reduced the fees. It now attracted engineering graduates who, having failed to secure a job, came to view the programme as a sure-fire way of landing an IT job. But YSM was never meant to be so.

However, we never lost the pedagogical advancements that we had made and used these methods to great success to again train a large number of engineering graduates from all over India. This time around, these graduates were fresh campus hires for companies such as IBM, Tech Mahindra, and so on, and went through five–six weeks of intensive entry level training programmes before they joined their employers for on-boarding and project deployment.

These short-duration success-based training programmes were paid for by the companies and formed a healthy revenue base for almost half a decade or more and were carried out almost on a nationwide basis. We had achieved a well fought turnaround.

Meanwhile, Globsyn Business School (GBS) became the main driving force behind our subsequent forays into the formal education sphere.

We roped in some of the best faculty in town and the first batch did exceedingly well as we doubled our intake to more than 100 students the subsequent year. Management education suited our style and we had the freedom to innovate and create a 'close-to-industry' programme that saw some of the biggest companies in India take part in the placement drive.

With GBS, we had insulated ourselves from being tied, by an umbilical cord as it were, to the fortunes of a single industry and broad-based our appeal.

GBS gave me the freedom to follow the academic trajectory of my students more closely, now that they were on campus for a better part of two years. It also gave me a platform to share my own entrepreneurial experiences with the young minds that dotted the campus. I did this by innovating a new concept that I christened 'Learn and Intern'.

During the earlier days, I held a minimum of four 'Learn and Intern' sessions with the students of every batch each year. These would be highly participative freewheeling sessions, some lasting up to three–four hours each, where we explored our own journey paths and ambitions.

These 'Learn and Intern' sessions proved to be highly motivating for the young minds, just out of college and about to embark upon their careers, and most of our alumni carried fond memories of these highly charged sessions.

I also followed up on my conviction, carried on from my IIT days, that there was more to be learned from outside the classroom than within the confines of its four walls.

The annual fest conducted by the school, christened Serendipity, was an attempt to move away from the practice of run-of-the-mill fests and I worked tirelessly alongside my students to transform the organisation and conduct of the event into a 'mini corporation'—one that mimicked a real-life corporation in all its aspects.

Designed as a two-day event, a select group of faculty members and I tutored students in forming the 'mini corporation' with a small starter fund from me. Students made up all the key departments, ranging from finance to marketing to HR and administration, along with special-purpose departments tasked to conduct the show.

The most brilliant of the students got to head each department aided by a slew of junior management positions all manned by students. The 'mini corporation' had its own CEO and maintained its own bank accounts.

It was great fun as the students conducted periodic reviews and performance appraisals, devised ingenious ways to raise funds by marketing event spots and the like, managing their finances and making countless presentations on their plans to make the event a success.

Serendipity gave everyone a voice and students were startled by their own self-discoveries. They measured their own success based on a predefined set of criteria; for instance, funds raised, cost management, people deployment and so forth and none of us from the management, including me, came between them and their 'mini corporation' except to play an advisory role when sought.

The fest culminated in students hosting their parents to dinner—a source of great pride for them. The quality and choice of cuisine, the size of the spread, everything depended on how well the students had managed their 'mini corporation' and the revenues generated to spend on a lavish evening.

'The smile on your parents' face should tell you all,' I told my students when they pestered me for feedback. Of course, I wore the biggest smile on those evenings.

⁂

Eleven

WITH GBS DOING WELL, we were steadily getting back on our feet, but I still had a mass of debt to pay off. As GBS started growing, I was forced to add a second floor to our campus, which added to my debt burden that now stood at around ₹8 crore—no mean sum for a company that was tottering out of the chasm.

With the moratorium period ending in March 2005, I didn't know where the money to start repaying my debt would come from when an old friend from my IIT days appeared out of the blue from Dubai to pay a courtesy visit.

It was as if he could read my mind as he looked down from the terrace and seeing the vast acreage of unused land adjoining our campus, innocently remarked, 'You are sitting on an NPA (non-performing asset), my friend.' We spent the rest of the evening discussing nothing of significance.

I went to bed that night with my friend's innocuous comment still ringing in my ears. By the time I woke up in the morning, I felt a new idea brewing inside me.

I fell back on my old Kolkata contacts and got my secretary to set up a meeting with one of the largest real estate developers in the city.

I had come to know Pradeep Sureka from my days when I was out in the market hunting for funds for the Infinity project. By late 2003 and early 2004, his group had grown to become a powerful real estate player in Kolkata and had built a number of landmarks around the city, including the iconic Park Plaza and Duckback House.

After some protracted negotiations, we finally agreed on an amicable share-holding pattern for a new joint venture that we launched to develop the approximately 2.5 acres of prime real estate that Globsyn had. We named our new project Globsyn Crystals, with twin towers creating more than 6,00,000 square feet of ultra-modern workspace.

With the Globsyn Crystals deal firmly stitched up, it gave me another opportunity after Infinity to position and market the project differently— an aspect of marketing that did not come naturally to pure-play real estate developers, though I must hasten to add that things have changed of late with housing projects taking on the lead.

We billed Globsyn Crystals as a 'work habitat' aimed at the 21st century knowledge-worker. With the knowledge economy ushering in a paradigm shift in working practices where 24×7 working cycles were natural, I felt that youngsters needed to bring 'work' and 'life' under a single roof and this singular aspect dominated both the architecture and design of the project.

In Globsyn Crystals, I also got a godsent opportunity to wipe off the entire debt burden that threatened to choke my growing company. It was another matter that I had to off load a significant part of my stake in the project at rock-bottom prices.

I remember telling some of my senior management staff the evening that I received an all-paid clearance from the bank, 'We are now debt-free guys, and I leave for the US a happy man with no regrets.'

I left a few days later for my heart bypass surgery in the US, content in the feeling that I had left a debt-free company for my people should, God forbid, something happen to me.

✍

I have known Bikram for more than three decades now. Popularly known as BDG, he, along with Dadan Bhai, created waves in the IT industry by launching low-cost PCs and doing the early IPO among IT companies. The product made a splash in 1990 at the CSI held in Kolkata, the biggest exhibition of IT products. I remember the huge jazzy pavilion of PCL, with BDG in all whites, and gold chain, imitating Bappi Lahiri. It was to BDG's credit that he was able to persuade Michael Dell and bring the iconic brand to India, another rarity as India was nowhere in the IT world those days. Going on, he bet big on Bengal with his venture, Globsyn, when no one was willing to touch the east.

He is a great lover of the golden oldies, especially songs by Kishore Kumar, which he himself also loves to sing. Right from his college days, he has been a theatre buff. He not only used to see plays, but also acted in and directed a number of them.

Pradeep Gupta
(Chairman, CyberMedia)

Twelve

By 2008–09, I HAD MANAGED to attract and retain a lot of bright talent at Globsyn and we were arguably one of the best teams in our business in east India. This was also one of the fastest growth periods for Globsyn, post our YSM days, and Globsyn Business School grew by leaps and bounds.

As we grew, we got more ambitious and introduced more specialised programmes in management. This time around, we chose to partner with some of the world's best universities and educational institutions, and offered specialised programmes in international finance and business.

It was around that time that I happened to meet Mr Jawhar Sircar, an incisive and highly erudite IAS officer who, as the principal secretary in the West Bengal government, had introduced several wide-ranging reforms in the higher and technical education sector in the face of stiff opposition from powerful unions and other entrenched groups with their own vested interests.

Mr Sircar subsequently went on to become the chairman of Prasar Bharati, India's largest public broadcasting agency, and held this post from February 2012 to October 2016. We still remain great friends.

As we sat in his office, discussing the future of my education venture and the outlook for higher education in the state, he told me something that had me thinking for a long time. 'Bikram,' he said, 'the way I look at it, as long as you are not an AICTE-approved institution, you will not be viewed as a mainstream guy and will always have to operate in the periphery of the education system. But if you do, you have it in you to build the first world class private management institute out of Bengal.' AICTE is the All-India Council for Technical Education.

We were doing well as an autonomous institution, albeit without formal accreditation, and I enjoyed the degree of freedom that it gave us to keep our institution closely aligned with the evolving market scenario. But Mr Sircar's statement hit me hard and I got myself to seriously investigate the possibilities of getting our business school formally accredited.

My initial plan was to get our Salt Lake campus accredited, but I found the going tough because of a number of seemingly archaic regulatory hurdles and rules. This, in turn, forced my hand to move the main campus to the outskirts of Kolkata.

This time around, Globsyn had built enough reserves to buy about three acres of land a few kilometres away from Joka, made famous by the Indian Institute of Management Kolkata.

Thus came to be born Globsyn's Knowledge Campus, but I soon found myself in debt again as I had to approach our bankers to extend some sizeable debt funds that went into prepping the land and building the three-storeyed campus.

By 2014, we finally moved into the new campus lock, stock and barrel. Prior to that, since early 2010, we had been operating from both our campuses, with our Knowledge Campus running the first of our pilot AICTE-accredited batches.

By 2012, it had become apparent that running two campuses was proving to be a strain on our finances, compounded further by a sluggish Indian economy that had started affecting the quality of placements.

Having witnessed severer storms in my life and my Globsyn journey, this was just a minor headwind that needed to be weathered, but people close to me started getting flustered. To them, my debt burden and cost structure had taken on gargantuan proportions and some action, however drastic, needed to be taken.

For the first time in my life I had to witness my own experiential management idioms come face to face with the new management knowledge that the new generation of youth believed in.

There was no right or wrong in this debate except that a singular path had to be chosen. To me, facing up to a storm and coming through it with a mix of grit, resilience and risk-taking contrasted sharply with the new generation's careful reading of the risks, assiduously developing spreadsheet scenarios and voting for a path that seemed more stable and prudent. But spreadsheets, like crystal ball gazing, never tell the full story.

To me, risk-taking and cost-cutting had been always a fine balancing act and I always sided with 'risk' rather than embark upon a purely 'cost' based approach to business. By siding heavily with the latter meant losing talent as much as losing mind share.

Businesses are known by the talent they hire and retain. As with every other aspect of life, it is always the select 10–15 per cent of people, across rank and function, who bring energy, dedication and an unflinching loyalty to a business, helping translate an entrepreneur's vision into reality. The rest merely help in sustaining the momentum of the business. The ability to recognise this core philosophy dictates our path more than the sum of numbers and spreadsheets.

As time went by, I finally capitulated to the softer and safer path and shut down our Salt Lake campus for good and made the Knowledge Campus our new home for our education business.

For someone not used to making too many compromises in life, the decision did not rest lightly on my shoulders as I flung myself back to reinvigorating the school.

As the years rolled on, we have witnessed an upturn in each of our businesses.

Our business school, now comfortable in its new campus and the environs that it found itself in, achieved its second major accreditation success in 2017 with its Post Graduate Diploma in Management (PGDM) programme being accredited by the National Board of Accreditation (NBA), India's premier accreditation body; we had achieved AICTE-accreditation way back in 2011.

With its series of innovative interventions GBS has in many ways introduced a new dimension to management education where 'Beyond Education' has become a way of life for GBS students.

Again, what started out as an 'idea' in 2001 has today grown to be among the top business schools in east India and figures among the top 6 per cent of business schools in India with NBA-accreditation for their PGDM programmes. Rahul is now driving the education business development.

Our software business that was gradually finding its feet back again has witnessed a healthy spurt in growth. Romit, the younger of the twins, has since taken over its operations and the newly christened company, Third Life, is growing at more than 100 per cent on a yearly basis while rapidly expanding its employee base and client relationships.

Technology and skills-driven training continue to be among Globsyn's strong domain strengths. Globsyn was among the early pioneers to participate in the skills development initiatives launched by the central government and figured prominently among the first joint venture partners of NSDC (National Skill Development Corporation; the nodal skill development organisation formed by the central government and industry bodies) in east India.

With close to 200 centres nationally and relationships with an equal number of engineering colleges, Globsyn has adapted its hugely popular Software Finishing School pedagogical system to train budding engineers on the latest set of IT technologies, helping bridge the gap between formal education and the needs of the evolving workplace. Rahul, the elder of the twins, runs this vertical and has taken on the mantle for its growth.

Not the one to rest on our laurels, Globsyn's education wing has recently applied for and received the necessary clearances to launch its own law school. Christened Globsyn Law School (GLS), I look upon it to develop and grow itself to be yet another milestone in my more than three decades of entrepreneurial journey.

My entrepreneurial journey, as perhaps all such journeys are, has been made up of huge highs and grim troughs. But I have enjoyed every moment of this lifelong journey of learning, as I picked up new skills along the way, skills that I never knew I possessed.

Learning never really stops for an entrepreneur and shouldn't for any one of us, as I keep reminding my people: 'Every six months, I come to the startling realisation how little I knew just six months back!'

The Infinity building under construction in Calcutta (now Kolkata) in 1996

*The then West Bengal Chief Minister Jyoti Basu at the
launch of the Infinity building in Calcutta (2000)*

Launch party of Infinity.
From right to left: Nandan Bhattacharya, Managing Director, Webel; S.N. Roy, former Chief Secretary, Government of West Bengal; Bikram Dasgupta; and Malay Kumar De, current Chief Secretary, Government of West Bengal

The completed Infinity project in Kolkata

The then West Bengal Chief Minister Jyoti Basu launches Bikram's first book, Minds on Fire, *in Kolkata (1999)*

Bikram releases the book, The Future of India: Politics, Economics and Governance, *written by former RBI Governor, Bimal Jalan, in Kolkata (2005)*

An artist's impression of the Globsyn Crystals complex in Kolkata

Bikram launches the Globsyn Crystals project in Kolkata.
Also seen are West Bengal's IT Minister Manab Mukherjee and West Bengal's
Principal Secretary, IT, G.D. Gautama (2006)

An artist's impression of the Globsyn Knowledge Campus, Kolkata

Governing Council of Globsyn Business School.
Seated from left to right: Praveen Gandhi, Pradip Kar, P.K. Ghosh, Arjun Malhotra,
Bikram Dasgupta, R.C. Bhattacharya, Samir Ghosh and Ramesh Maheswari

*Working professionals with their certificates after undergoing
skills training at Globsyn (2014)*

*Bikram chats with a member of an old-age home adopted by his foundation Kalyani,
named in memory of his late mother, in Kolkata (2013)*

Bikram with his twin sons Romit and Rahul

Bikram with his granddaughter Mishka and wife Ranjana (2017)

Bikram's innovations

Moving On

It is what you read when you don't have to that determines what you will be when you can't help it...

—Oscar Wilde

O<small>F ALL THE BOOKS THAT I HAVE READ</small>, Khalil Gibran's *The Prophet* and Richard Bach's *Jonathan Livingston Seagull* remain my all-time favourites and I shall never tire of reading them, no matter how many times I might have read the books.

Both books have something magical about them, as perhaps all great reads are, with each reading presenting me with new insights and firing up my imagination. This is the defining character of good books; they do something inexplicable, helping heave oneself from one's own preconceived limitations of mind, body and soul.

The famous American author and screenwriter Ray Bradbury's tribute to Bach's *Jonathan Livingston Seagull* is perhaps closest to my own sentiment as he goes on to say, 'Richard Bach with this book does two things. He gives me Flight. He makes me Young. For both I am grateful.' As am I.

Bradbury's eulogy would work equally prophetically for Gibran's *The Prophet*, which was written some decades earlier.

Like Jonathan Livingston Seagull, living the humdrum life in a flock does not interest me. The urge to fly higher, better and faster was an infective affliction that I perhaps caught during my days at IIT and one that has stayed with me forever.

The craving to fly faster and better, transcending the inherent limitations of wing design, was a mysterious puzzle to a large number of people who made up my world. They mistook it as arrogance, driven perhaps by an irrational ego.

But for me it was the sheer exhilaration of being able to break the shackles of what kept the flocks moored to their placid existence that mattered. Thus, like Jonathan, who, having discovered that there was more to living than mindlessly flying from shore to sea, took to educating the flock on this newfound knowledge, I too, took my newfound awareness to the classroom.

In the over 100 hours of Learn and Intern sessions that I have taken in my business school, I have held forth, to a new generation of gulls, the example of Jonathan Livingston Seagull; the seagull that could break the fetters of its flock's thinking and the design of its wings to fly higher, faster and better than anyone else.

This brings me to dwell on today's youth who are finding it increasingly difficult to manage the challenges of living in a world awash in a 'diarrhoea of information'—an incisive observation made by our late Prime Minister P.V. Narasimha Rao, during his tea invite.

Today, the youth inhabits a world full of textual, visual and sensual distractions, flitting from topic to topic, idea to idea and activity to activity. Sure, it is a much richer and informed world, but there lurks in the shadows a far serious risk.

The risk of getting lost in the labyrinth of information and falling prey to distractions is only growing by the day. Distractions brought about by money, early taste of power and changing work habits are emerging as serious barriers for large swathes of youth from striving for excellence.

They would do well to remember what Gibran says in *The Prophet*...

The hidden wellspring of your soul must needs rise and run murmuring to the sea; And the treasure of your infinite depths would be revealed to your eyes.

Generations inhabit and inherit vastly different worlds. If our fathers' generation was consumed with India wresting her independence from Britain, our generation has perhaps devoted much of its energy to heave ourselves out from being the citizenry of a third world country to one of the fastest growing world economies.

Our next and future generations would inhabit a world where the marvel of quantum physics has made distances irrelevant; the information revolution has paved the way for a more aware and informed citizenry and social and work life, as we know it, will come to be increasingly automated.

The growth in the power of artificial intelligence (AI) will dramatically alter both our work and social spaces. Fed by gigantic vats of data, information-processing machines will learn and adapt at a furious pace, helping humans break their inherent limitations in ingesting and processing information making them better, and better capable of arriving at highly developed decision models.

This will affect how we shop and drive, homes that we inhabit and transform our existing understanding of human and machine productivity. The Second Machine Age will necessitate bringing in fundamental changes in our education system, calling for new skills to be developed. Our youth will get better at multi-tasking, aided in large measure by machines and perhaps be sharper and more intelligent than us.

As I step into my sunset years, I look forward to the thrill of immersing myself in my new vision for my business school and an AI-driven world, but as Jonathan, I live to tell the youth to believe in the power of their wings; to fly faster, higher and better than they ever imagined that they could...

> 'The teacher who walks in the shadow of the temple, among his followers, gives not of his wisdom but rather of his faith and his lovingness. If he is indeed wise he does not bid you enter the house of his wisdom, but rather leads you to the threshold of your own mind'.

> —Khalil Gibran (*The Prophet*)

Acknowledgements

The book that you are holding in your hands wouldn't have been possible but for my family, friends and acquaintances who have been a constant source of inspiration, acted as my muse and who delved into their own memory banks to ferret out incidents and events of our lives spent together. They have been the source of my own education in life and my journey would have remained an insipid one without them. This book has happily bestowed upon me the cheeriest task of thanking them all, now and forever.

This book is also, in many ways, my tribute to the mentors in my life, Shiv Nadar, Arjun Malhotra, (the late) Dadan Bhai, (the late) Amit Dutta Gupta, and V. Balagopalan—my first boss.

I apologise if I have missed anyone. It is not a conscious act but one that I can only attribute to a failing memory as I advance in age. I have chosen to list the names in alphabetical order and have largely stuck to the phase in which they have appeared in my life.

Snehamay Nag and Sohan Hatangadi, fellow Vizagites, who made my life in Vizag an eventful one. Ashok Soota, Ashwini Talwar, Krish Vijayaraghavan, Pradeep Gupta, Pradeep Kar, Pravin Gandhi, Rajendra S. Pawar, and Vijay K. Thadani without whose camaraderie my journey from HCL to PCL and finally flying solo with Globsyn wouldn't have been half as exciting.

This brings me to the pleasant task of acknowledging, with deep gratitude, the time and effort put in by Supratim Kar in helping me write the book and giving it the life and character it has. Thank you, Supratim.

I would also like to thank and acknowledge Rupa Publications India, especially Dibakar Ghosh, Rupa's Editorial Director, for giving me the platform to share my story with the world.

I would be amiss if I fail to mention Ranjana, my wife; my sons Romit and Rahul; Sharon Gomes, my personal secretary for many years, and Shabbir Akhtar for helping me and Supratim manage the demanding back office requirements that went into bringing this book to life.